Become Proficient in
Speaking and Writing
GOOD ENGLISH

V&S PUBLISHERS

Published by

F-2/16, Ansari Road, Daryaganj, New Delhi-110002
☎ 011-23240026, 011-23240027 • *Fax* 011-23240028
Email info@vspublishers.com • *Website* www.vspublishers.com

Regional Office Hyderabad
5-1-707/1, Brij Bhawan (Beside Central Bank of India Lane)
Bank Street, Koti, Hyderabad - 500 095
☎ 040-24737290
E-mail vspublishershyd@gmail.com

Branch Office Mumbai
Godown # 34 at The Model Co-Operative Housing, Society Ltd.,
"Sahakar Niwas", Ground Floor, Next to Sobo Central, Mumbai - 400 034
☎ 022-23510736
E-mail vspublishersmum@gmail.com

Follow us on

All books available at **www.vspublishers.com**

© **Copyright:** V&S PUBLISHERS
ISBN 978-93-813843-8-1
Edition 2014

The Copyright of this book, as well as all matter contained herein (including illustrations) rests with the Publisher. No person shall copy the name of the book, its title design, matter and illustrations in any form and in any language, totally or partially or in any form. Anybody doing so shall face legal action and will be responsible for damages.

Printed at Param Offseters Okhla New Delhi-110020

Dedication

*In Memory of
My Grandfather
Hari Mohan Mathur
Gold Medalist in English Literature
from Agra University*

PREFACE

It is emphasised that all compositions should be able to express clearly what the writer wishes to convey—be it a letter, an article, a report, or even a book. Good writing takes into account proper organisation of the written matter, good sentence construction, correct grammar, and suitable use of punctuation and other marks, besides several other parameters. A well-written and structured composition gives a favourable impression of the writer to the reader. Conversely, a badly presented material may confuse or distract the reader, even dissuading him from reading. I have been conscious of the facts mentioned above while preparing "BECOME PROFICIENT IN WRITING & SPEAKING GOOD ENGLISH."

Not so long ago a writer used a pen and paper to write in long hand or type out a communication, but the modern author has recourse to a word processor on the computer. This makes their task simpler as they could type out the points or even thoughts on the processor and organize them into a whole document by adding and deleting, by arranging and rearranging the matter and suitable editing without much hassle. However, the spell-check device needs care because most computers follow the American usage while the British style is acceptable in India. But in most software it can be altered to British usage by going to Language option in Tools on the Menu Bar.

Any one aspiring to write good prose must have on his desk at least one dictionary from each side of the Atlantic for British and American spellings, as usage of some words and expressions are different between the two. This work follows the British style. A thesaurus is also very useful, as it not only serves to increase one's vocabulary and helps in avoiding repetition of the same word by giving synonyms but it also helps in choosing the right word that conveys the exact shade of thought or meaning that one wishes to convey.

This book would not have been possible without the active cooperation of my father, Mr. S. M. Mathur. He helped me in my research, in finding appropriate examples, and in several other ways. My words of thanks cannot adequately express my indebtness to him.

• **ARCHANA MATHUR**

The Need of
"GOOD ENGLISH"

English : An International Language

English today is the lingua franca of international communication, of diplomacy, of commerce, or just of interaction between people of different nationalities—even between Indians speaking different regional languages. Because of its universal acceptance the European Union has adopted it as its official language though it has appointed a commission to simplify it. It is the preferred language of computers—over eighty percent of all websites are in English. Even highly chauvinistic societies that are jealously proud of their language—such as the French, the Russian, the Chinese and the Japanese—are perforce learning it because of its world-wide standing and importance. Non-English speaking people, if they wish to bring their scientific, technical and academic studies to the notice of the world at large, prefer to publish their work in this language. Indians across the globe have made their mark in the field of information technology and other scientific disciplines because of their proficiency in English.

Why was this Book Created?

Practically all higher teaching and research in management, medicine, science and technology subjects are carried out in English, not only because most books and journals in these subjects and their various disciplines are in this language but also because it is the language of virtually all internal and international business and commerce communications. Most of the scientific, technical and business terminology is English-language based. It is therefore, important to understand all aspects of the language and to write not only grammatically correct prose but also to organize and present it in a cogent manner which appeals to the reader. There are also some conventions in style that are required to be followed for proper presentation. That is the reason that this book was created.

The output of the printed word in the English language, right from books, magazines and newspapers to posters and handbills in India, is simply phenomenal. It becomes imperative, therefore, to be proficient in English and to write it correctly and idiomatically. Badly written and constructed material is not uncommon—mistakes in spelling, grammar and incorrect use of words abound. It must be admitted though that the English language poses several problems in syntax and usage that sometimes baffle writers, not only those whose mother tongue is not English but also people who speak and use the language from birth. But by following the generally accepted rules and conventions many pitfalls can be avoided. There is a plethora of foreign publications on various aspects of correct and good writing but hardly any that focuses on the requirement of the Indian writer. The aim and scope of this work is to make a contribution towards removal of this deficiency. That is another important reason that this book was created.

How is this Dictionary Unique in Presentation?

It is not a text that deals with theoretical aspects of writing but offers practical advice in an alphabetical format for writing proper and attractive prose to improve one's communication skills. The topics cover commonly made mistakes and confusing set of words, proper and effective use of figures of speech, various aspects of grammar and syntax, foreign language words commonly used in English, besides many other aspects of attractive writing.

This book, *'Become Proficient in Writing and Speaking Good English'*, guides the user to communicate effectively by using correct and idiomatic language. This is to be achieved by building the understanding and knowledge of the language and by discussing its various aspects, including correct usage, origin and source of words. It also gives some insight into aspects of the language that would help in writing good prose. The topics are arranged alphabetically for easy reference. The entries have adequate and appropriate examples. It would be a good idea to carefully go through all the entries: this would alert the readers to steer away from commonly made mistakes and to direct them to use the language properly.

Eight appendices are included to enrich the vocabulary and knowledge of the reader. They contain lists of groups of words and terms that are likely to be useful in expanding one's vocabulary and their appropriate usage for better communication.

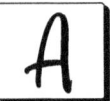

A and **An** are indefinite articles.

'A' is generally used before nouns starting with a consonant or consonantal sound.
> *A* cow gives milk.
> *A* pen is used for writing.

'An' is used before nouns, starting with vowels or vowel sounds.
> *An* elephant was used to move timber.
> *An* umbrella gives protection from the sun and the rain.
> *An* hour a day is sufficient to learn the subject.
> She is *an* honest woman.
> She is *an* M.P. [But: She is *a* Member of Parliament.]
> She works for *an* NGO [But: She works for *a* Non-Government Organization.]

'A' is used before the words starting with a vowel but having a consonant sound.
> *A* one-rupee coin.
> *A* useful book.

'An' is also used before a word where the initial constant 'h' is silent before a vowel.
> *An* hour a day is sufficient to learn the subject.
> He is *an* honorary member of the club.

But: a word beginning with 'h' where it is pronounced takes 'a':
> There is also *a* hotel in the village.
> He is *a* historian.

A, as a prefix to certain verbs, forms its unstressed variant. Some examples are given here.

abed = in bed
> She saw the kids *abed* before leaving for the movie.

afloat = in floating condition
> The life jacket kept him *afloat*.

aglow = radiate with light or excitement
> She was *aglow* with pride on her achievement.

amoral = lacking moral sensibility or unconcerned whether something is right or wrong
> Children are *amoral*, and often cannot distinguish between a right or wrong action.

anew = once again
  Having failed once, he will try to climb the Everest *anew*.

apolitical = having no interest in politics
  Although born in a political family he is *apolitical*.

awake = wake up, rouse from sleep
  He was jolted *awake* when the first shock of the quake hit his house.

await = wait for
  The students eagerly *awaited* their result.

awash = covered or flooded with water
  The beach was *awash* with tiny shells as the tide hit it.

A number of... Here is confusing grammar. Though the subject, *number*, is in a singular form it is so strongly plural in meaning that it takes a plural verb.
  A number of children *are* absent today.
  A number of men *were* arrested for rioting.
  A number of seats *are* still available in the school.
  A number of shops *were* gutted in the fire.

However, when used with definite article 'the', *number* takes a singular verb.
  The number of children absent today *has* come down.
  The number of men arrested for rioting *is* only ten.
  The number of reserved seats for the handicapped *has* been increased.
  The number of shops looted during rioting *is* not known.

Abbreviated Latin Words and Phrases. Several foreign words and phrases are abbreviated in English writing and used widely. They are generally from the Latin and are not italicized. The common abbreviations with original Latin and their English meanings are given below:

Abbreviation	Latin word(s)	English meaning
A.D.	*Anno Domini*	of the Christian era
Ad lib.	*ad libitum*	improvised, without preparation
c./ca.	*circa*	about a certain date
cf.	*confer*	compare
C.V.	*curriculum vitae*	brief account of ones' previous career
e.g.	*exempli gratia*	for example
et al.	*et alii*	and others
etc.	*etcetera*	and so forth
et seq.	*et sequential*	and following pages/matter
ibid	*ibidem*	in the same work, book, chapter, or passage
id.	*idem*	the same author, or the same word
inf.	*infra*	below
N.B.	*nota bene*	take careful notice

non seq.	*non sequitur*	it does not follow
op. sit.	*opere citato*	in the work already cited
P.S.	*postscriptum*	post-script
P.S.S.	*postscriptuma*	post-scripts [plural]
q.v.	*quod vide*	which see
R.I.P.	*requiescat* (pl. *reqiescant*)	rest in peace (after death)
R.S.V.P.	*respondez s'il vous plait*	please answer (the invitation)
sup.	*supra*	above
v./vs.	*versus*	against
viz.	*videlict*	namely

Abbreviated Phrases. It has lately become popular in correspondence and journalistic writing to use abbreviations for some popular phrases. They are written with or without punctuation (generally the latter) and each letter is pronounced individually.

a.k.a. / aka = also known as
Dacoit Ambika Patel *aka* Thokia was killed recently in a police encounter.

a.s.a.p. / asap = as soon as possible
Please reply *asap* as the matter is urgent.

AWOL / awol) = Absent Without Official Leave (without notice or permission but not with intent to desert) [military term, used also in general]
The office could not work full strength as five employees went *AWOL* last week.

PDQ = pretty damn quick (immediately) [Naval jargon, also used in general]
I want this letter delivered to the client *PDQ*.

w.e.f. = with effect from
She will take charge of the Principlal *w.e.f.* next July.

Abbreviation is the shortened form of a word or words that consists of the initial letter or letters and is generally punctuated by stops, though there is a current tendency to ignore the stops. Names of practically all multi-word organizations, products, phrases are abbreviated in common usage, usually in capitals. Little-known abbreviations used in a communication should be used only after the full form in written first and the abbreviation indicated within parentheses. Titles, ranks, academic degrees, compass directions are commonly abbreviated. They are different from **acronyms** and letter symbols. [See also **Contraction** and **Elision**]

Abbreviations as contractions. Some abbreviations are actually contractions without an apostrophe even though the first and last letters of the word have been used. They generally take a stop though there is increasing tendency to omit it.

Dept.	=	Department
Dr.	=	Doctor
Govt.	=	Government
Jr.	=	Junior
Mr.	=	Mister
Mt.	=	Mount / Mountain
Rd.	=	Road
Sr.	=	Senior
St.	=	Saint

Abbreviations of diurnal time. The correct way to write abbreviation of time is in lower case, but capitals, normal or small, are sometimes used, particularly by the Americans. Forenoon and afternoon abbreviations are always in capitals.

a.m.
p.m..
F.N.
A.N.

Abbreviations with a slash. Some abbreviations take a slash.

a/c	=	account
c/o	=	care of
d/o	=	daughter of
i/c	=	incharge
S/B	=	savings bank
s/o	=	son of

Abbreviations, their plural. Plurals of most abbreviations are formed by suffixing the usual 's' in lower case. In some cases the plurals are indicated by repetition of the abbreviated letter. The styles of capitalization are shown in the examples:

cc	...	copies
ff	...	following pages
JJ	...	Judges
MSS	...	manuscripts
pp	...	pages

Abridge and **condense** are both verbs having the meaning of 'to shorten or compress'. *Abridge* has the fine sense of 'shortening a text by omission of words without losing the sense', while condense implies 'to reduce to fewer words a longer document or speech'.

Both the words can often be used as synonyms in writing.

A new abridged / condensed version of the novel has come out.
The novel has been abridged but has lost its charm.
The condensed version of the novel has been so well done that it is like reading the original.

A

Absurdities in written and spoken English involve the use of many modifiers that occur commonly. They are **solecisms** that must be avoided at all cost.

Most unique [Unique is 'one and only one of a kind and having no equal', then it cannot be the 'most'.]

Absolutely perfect ['perfect' indicates 'something faultless' so 'absolutely', is redundant.]

More better ['better' is already a comparative of *good,* so 'more' cannot be an additional comparative. It is **tautology.**]

Acknowledgement or **acknowledgment.** Both the spellings (with or without 'e' after 'acknowledge') are permissible.

Acronyms are shortened forms or abbreviations composed from the initial letters of other words or phrases, and are written without punctuation and are pronounced as words. Some acronyms have now become regular words.

laser	*l*ight *a*mplification by *s*imulate *e*mission *r*adiation
radar	*r*adio *d*etection *a*nd *r*anging
sonar	*s*ound *n*avigation *a*nd *r*anging
scuba	*s*elf-*c*ontained *u*nderwater *b*reathing *a*pparatus

Acronyms formed from names of some organizations were originally written all in capitals but generally now only the initial letter is capitalized.

Barc	*B*habha *A*tomic *R*esearch *C*entre
Isro	*I*ndian *S*pace *R*esearch *O*rganization
Noida	*N*ew *O*khla *I*ndustrial *D*evelopment *A*uthority
Unesco	*U*nited *N*ations *E*ducational and *S*cientific *O*rganization
Unicef	*U*nited *N*ations *I*nternational *C*hildren's *E*mergency *F*und

Other types of acronyms are in capital letters only but are pronounced as words.

AIDS	*a*cquired *i*mmune *d*eficiency *s*yndrome
DOS	*d*isc *o*perating *s*ystem
NATO	*N*orth *A*tlantic *T*reaty *O*rganisation
RAM	*r*andom *a*ccess *m*emory

A.D. and **B.C.** These two abbreviations refer to historical dates with reference to the Christian era. *A.D.* is Latin for *Anno Domini,* meaning 'in year of the Lord' indicating that the date(s) is (are) during the Christian era; it is written <u>before</u> the date. *B.C.* means 'before Christ' and is placed <u>after</u> the date indicating that it is before the Christian era. Sometimes, these abbreviations are not punctuated and are written or printed in capitals. [Note: These related abbreviations are from two different languages, Latin and English]

Mt Vesuvius erupted in *A.D. 79* and the cities of Pompeii and Herculaneum were buried under its lava. [A.D. is written <u>before</u> the date.]

The Mauryan empire flourished between *321-185 B.C.* [B.C. is written <u>after</u> the date.]

Adage. See **Proverb...**

Adapt and **adopt** are two similar verbs with different meanings and are likely to be confused in usage. *Adapt* implies 'to modify or alter according to changing circumstances'. *Adopt* means 'to take into relationship or take another idea' that may have originated elsewhere.
> Many Europeans have *adapted* themselves to the harsh Indian summer by *adopting* Indian dress.
> Several appliances have been *adapted* to work on 220 volts instead of 110 volt as in America.
> Some European celebrities have *adopted* African children recently.
> The law was *adopted* after a few amendments.

Adjacent; adjoining; subjacent. *Adjacent* means 'near to each other', but *adjoining* indicates joined together' as by a common wall. The meanings of these two adjectives are distinct but sometimes the two words could be interchanged. *Subjacent* has the special implication of 'situated under or below'.
> My house is *adjacent* to the Hanuman temple but there is a lane in-between.
> My house is *adjoining* his house, only a low wall separating the two.
> The Doon Valley is *subjacent* to the Mussoorie Hills.

Adjectives from proper names. Some people have given their names to special qualities or philosophies attributed to them which go by their names which are capitalized in writing.

Churchilian is an adjective formed from the famous British statesman Winston Churchill for his great oratory that he embellished by using rhetoric and flourish.
> In India Atal Behari Vajpayee is considered a great orator for his *Churchillean* flourish of rhetorical language.

Gandhian is an adjective formed from the name of Mahatma Gandhi which coveys a way of life of austerity, honesty, truth and nonviolence.
> Martin Luther King, Jr., was the embodiment of *Gandhian* principles in the United States.

Machiavellian has become an adjective to enunciate the principles of conduct laid down by the Italian politician Machiavelli marked by cunning, scheming or unscrupulous duplicity or bad faith in politics and business.
> The *Machiavellian* cunning of some Indian politicians has resulted in fragmentation of the Indian society as never before.

Nehruvian is an adjective formed from the name of Jawaharlal Nehru who advocated socialism in India after Independence.
> *Nehruvian* model of development envisaged control of all economic activities by the state.

Orwellian has become an adjective after an English author George Orwell who propounded a policy of control by propaganda, misinformation, and denial of the truth of colonial oppression which he felt was for the good of the oppressed people.

>Though the British have left some African dictators have used *Orwellian* techniques to oppress their people.

Advice; advise. These two words often cause some confusion. But if you remember the difference in pronunciation, you are not likely to make a mistake. *Advice* is a noun and means 'opinion or guidance given', and is pronounced with a soft 'c'. *Advise* is a verb with the meaning of 'to give advice or suggestion' or 'counsel', and is pronounced with a 'z' sound.

>He withdrew his case on the *advice* of his lawyer.
>His lawyer *advised* him to withdraw the case.

Affect; effect. There is often confusion about the right use of these two words. *Affect* is primarily a verb that means 'to produce a feeling' or 'to influence'. *Effect* is a noun that means 'result'; 'consequence' or 'impression', but is also a verb to mean 'to bring about' or 'to accomplish'.

>Alcohol *affects* different people in different ways. [verb]
>She was greatly *affected* by the condolence messages from everyone. [verb]
>Everyone in the room is *affected* by his chain smoking. [verb]
>The disease has *affected* the movement of her hands. [verb]
>People have given up alcohol as the *effect* of Baba Ramdeo's teachings. [noun]
>The *effect* of alcohol on some people is to make them rowdy [noun]
>Police *effected* the arrest of the chain-snatcher after a long chase. [verb]
>The order is likely to have no *effect* on the free sale of beer. [verb]

Afrikaans words. Several words in the English language are taken from Afrikaans—the official language of the Republic of South Africa—a language derived from Dutch.

>*apartheid* = segregation of races
>*spoor* = track; foot-print
>*trek* = arduous journey especially on foot
>*veld/veldt* = uncultivable grassland

Agenda. This is the plural of *agendum* but has been widely used as singular, and a plural *agendas* has been coined. So instead of swimming against the popular usage there is no alternative but to accept *agenda* as singular.

>The *agenda* for the meeting was drawn up ten days in advance.
>The *agendas* of all the meetings should be sent well in advance.

Allegory is a form of extended **metaphor** in which fictional things in a story, poem or picture are introduced to interpret truths or generalisations with underlying meanings.

Alliteration is the use of two or more words in close succession in a sentence beginning with the same letter or sound, usually a consonant. The use of alliteration sometimes gives a lyrical feel to the prose.
>He keeps cool, calm and collected in an emergency.
>Betty's bitter butter is better than sally's
>She sells sea shells on the sea shore. [Also a tongue-twister]

Alright; all right. Allright is a short, combined form of two words, *all* and *right* . The purist frown on it and write it in two separate words, *all right*, but *alright*, as one word, is in wide use particularly in speech.
>It is *alright* for you to write your paper in Hindi.
>It is *all right* for you to write your paper in Hindi.

Also; too. Both adverbs have the same meaning in the sense of 'besides' or 'likewise'. When used at the end of a sentence in this sense it sometimes follows a comma. 'Too' also has the meaning of 'excessive'.
>She would *also* like to take part in the school drama.
>She would like to take part in the school drama, *too*.
>He wants to sell off his TV and the VCR, *too*.
>The house is *too* large for a single family. [excessive]
>He has gone *too* far this time in blaming others for his mistakes. [more than what is desirable]

Altogether; all together. The two forms are often confused. *Altogether* means 'entirely', 'wholly', 'completely'. In a special informal sense, it means 'nude' preceded by 'the'. The phrase a*ll together* has the meaning of 'in one place or in a group'.
>The trip cost five thousand rupees *altogether*. [entirely]
>The model posed in *the altogether*. [in the nude]
>The hikers meet at the forest lodge *all together*. [in one place, the lodge]
>The cricket team flew back *all together*. [in one group]

Although; Though. These two words cause some confusion when used in a sentence, but both are practically interchangeable except in certain cases. *Although* can be used anywhere in the sentence except at the end, but *though* can occur any where including the end of a sentence.
>*Although/Though* the train was crowded we found a seat.
>We found a seat *(al)though* the train was crowded.
>It's hard work, I enjoy it *though*.
>I will call on you soon, it will take a little while *though*.

There are some sentences, in which the two words can be interchanged. But in the following examples *though* cannot be replaced by *although*.
>I liked the book. I decided not to buy it *though*.
>He was behaving as *though* he owned the place.

I didn't show my feelings, happy *though* I was.

Altitude and **elevation** are nouns, both concerned with heights: *altitude* refers to 'vertical height above the sea level or land', and *elevation* to 'vertical height above a given level'.

> The *altitude* of Mt. Everest is 8850 metres above the sea level.
> India is planning to place a remote sensing satellite at an *altitude* of 600 km above the Earth.
> The maximum *elevation* allowed for a building in Lucknow is 30 metres.
> The *elevation* of the surrounding hills above the valley varies between 30 and 65 metres.

Alumnus; alumni; alumna; alumnae. These related words are frequently used in academic circles but often cause some confusion. *Alumnus* is singular, and *alumni* is plural for both the genders of former students. *Alumna* is female, singular, and *alumnae* is female plural.

> He/she is an *alumnus* of the Delhi University.
> The *alumni* of the English Department will have a get-together next Wednesday.
> She is an *alumna* of the Women's College, Varanasi.
> Several *alumnae* of the Women's College occupy important positions in the society today.

a.m.; p.m. *a.m.* is the abbreviation of Latin *ante meridiem* meaning 'before noon', and *p.m.* is the abbreviation of Latin *post meridiem* meaning 'afternoon'. These abbreviations are written in lower case following British usage, but the Americans write them in capitals, using small capitals in printing. It is redundant to write '10 a.m. in the morning', and '6 p.m. in the evening'.

> The classes will be held from 8.30 a.m. to 3.30 p.m.
> The eclipse will be visible between 3.27 and 5.42 p.m.

Amend; emend. With the same sound but slight alteration of the initial letter these two words mean the same 'change' but have different shades of meaning. *Amend* signifies a 'change or modification of a document, proposal, etc.', while *emend* means 'to correct or revise', generally a document or text. The derivatives of *amend* are *amendable* (adjective), *amender* (noun), and *amendment* (noun), and those of *emend* are *emendable* (adjective), and *emendation* (noun) (but not 'emendment').

> There is a proposal to *amend* the Constitution to provide for reservation to OBCs.
> The text of the book was *emended* to remove some offensive passages.
> The Supreme Court struck down the 39th Amendment and part of the 42nd Amendment of the constitution as violation of Basic Structure of the Constitution.
> The *emendation* of the text was done to improve the language.

American spelling. There are many words which are spelt differently by the Americans from the British. The dictionaries in American softwares spell words the American way, and the spell check of a computer may confuse the Indian user who follows the British spelling. If in doubt, a British dictionary should be consulted. The main entry of a word in American dictionaries follows the American style but may sometimes also print the British variant.

The use of the ending '-ise' versus '-ize' has been discussed elsewhere in this work. Some other differences in styles may be noted here. The British ending '-our' in American words is reduced to '-or', and '-re' to '-er'. Another American style is to spell some words with a single 'l' or 'm' while the British spelling has two. Some other American spellings tend to be phonetically simpler.

British	*American*
behaviour	behavior
colour	color
honour	honor
humour	humor
centre	center
metre	meter
theatre	theater
cunsellor	counselor
jeweller	jeweler
traveller	traveler
gemmology	gemology
programme	program
cheque	check
tyre	tire

American words. A large number of words originating from the United States have seeped into the English language. A few that are commonly encountered and are typical of American vocabulary are given here.

Band-Aid = makeshift solution
    Before the matter goes to the boss let's try a *band-aid* to repair the damage.

buddy = friend; companion
    He is a good *buddy* of mine.

caucus = a group of people united to promote a common cause
    There is a small *caucus* in the Congress that is opposed to aid to Pakistan

doodad / Doohickey = a small item whose common name is unknown or forgotten
    This *doodad/ doohickey* is useful for opening tin cans.

dude = dandy man; bloke
    This *dude* is very popular with the girls.

hunky-dory = quite satisfactory
    Everything is *hunky-dory* between them after the quarrel.

O.K. /OK/ okay = all right
    It is *O.K.* for you to sit here.

yucky = bad; offensive
    The food was so *yucky* that I threw-up.

Ampersand is the symbol **&,** which means 'and'. It is generally used in name of companies: *Sharma & Co. Ltd.* The symbol is many times used in a text which is wrong because in a text 'and' is to be written in full. Yes, if the name of the company occurs in a sentence and is part of the text then it may stand as such.
    I have agreed to meet him *&* give him lunch. [The symbol is improper]
    I have agreed to meet him and give him lunch. [Proper]
    Among the prominent exporters is *Sharma & Co.* whose office is nearby. [Proper]

And as conjunction is used to join sentences and should not start a new sentence according to purists. However, it is no longer frowned upon to start sentences with *And* (or **But** or **Because**).
    The board decided to condone the shortfall in attendance of the students. And the subsequent meeting of the Executive Council endorsed the decision .

And/ or. This usage for conveying the meaning of 'either or both' is quite popular and convenient, though it may be frowned upon by the purists.
    In the prevailing situation of unrest, the administration should be ready to deploy the police *and/or* the army.

The purist would like to recast the sentence as follows:
    In the prevailing situation of unrest, the administration should be ready to deploy *the police or the army or both.*

Doesn't the above sound stilted?

Angry at; angry with. The two expressions cause quite a bit of confusion. You can be angry at some event or thing, but you can be angry with only a person.
    They were *angry at* the poor arrangements made at the conference.
    She was *angry with* her husband for forgetting her birthday.

Ante-; anti-. These two prefixes are prone to common confusion. Ante- means 'before' while anti- means 'opposite' or 'against'.
    The order of arrest *antedates* the bail granted by the high court.
    The injuries on the head of the victim appear to be *ante-mortem*.
    Apply an *antiseptic* lotion to the injury.
    The *anti-Semitic* feeling in the Arab world is widespread.

Antithesis is a figure of speech in which rhetorical contrast of ideas is marked by parallelism of contrasted words, clauses or sentences.
    To err is human, to forgive divine. (Alexander Pope)
    If all the rubble is to be removed by the municipality *action, not words,* is required by the authorities.

The colonial powers *promised freedom but provided slavery.*
In life the *difficult and easy* complement each other.
In life *high and low* occur from time to time and one can't do anything.

Antonomasia is a figure of speech where a person or epithet is substituted for a proper name or thing indicating that the two share some common characters. [See also **Euphemism**]
> Abdul Gaffer Khan was known as Frontier Gandhi.
> Sarojni Naidu is often called the Nightingale of India.
> The Godavari River is dubbed as the Ganga of the South.
> He is as wise as Solomon. [after an ancient king of Israel]

Antonym is a word of opposite meaning. Here are a few common examples:
> Big — small
> Day — night
> Expensive — cheap
> Good — bad

Sometimes an antonym may be used in a negative sense to refer to the word whose antonym it is. (Compare: **litotes** in which an affirmative is expressed by the negative of the contrary.)
> He is *not* such a *small* boy that his school mates may tease him with impunity.
> It was *not* yet *night* and one could clearly see the house yonder.
> The book is *not* so *expensive* that a student can't buy it.
> It is *not* a *bad* idea to go to the hills during the summer vacations.

Aphorism is a short, pithy or terse statement or saying that is based on truth. It may be used with some effect to emphasise a point. (See also **Proverb**)
> An eye for an eye will make the whole world blind. (Mahatma Gandhi)
> One man's terrorist is another man's freedom fighter.

Apostrophe is a figure of speech in which an exclamatory passage in speech or poem is addressed to a person or personified thing.
> O *Liberty*, what things are done in thy name. (Thomas Carlyle)
> Fair daffodils, we weep to see/*You* haste away so soon. (Robert Herrick, *To Daffodils*)

Apostrophe is also a mark (') used to indicate omission of letter(s) or number(s).[See **Contraction of verb phrases, Contraction of year date,** and **Elision**] It also indicates the possessive case.
> You *can't* go to school today.
> The *'90s* saw increase in sale of cars in India.
> The date of her birth is 20th July *'92*.
> This is *Sharma's* car.

Apparent; evident; obvious. These three adjectives mean practically the same: 'clearly recognizable' or 'perceived'. *Apparent* and *obvious* describe what can be seen and is not concealed, and *evident* also has an element of mental perception.

> The *apparent* cause of the heart attack was the sudden death of her son in an accident.
> It is *evident* that her queer behaviour is due to mental stress.
> It is *evident* from the broken rear door that the thieves entered the house from that side.
> It is *obvious* from the broken rear door that the thieves entered from that side

Approximation and synonyms. There are several adverbs that are used to indicate fairly near the figure but not totally precise. *About* and *approximate* are quite similar in meaning of 'fairly accurate but not totally precise so'. *About* carries the sense that the figure approaches very nearly but not quite and that it could be somewhat less, while *approximately* gives the sense that the figures are closer to the fact. *Almost* carries the sense that it approaches the figure very nearly but not quite and that it could be somewhat lesser. *Around* is somewhat more imprecise but closer to exactness. *Nearly* is closer to almost but introduces an element of slightly greater certainty, almost but not quite. *Roughly* indicates approximation but introduces greater uncertainty. *Some* introduces uncertainty, considerable but unspecified, unknown and undetermined.

> She was *about* 80 when she died.
> The cost of the new computer is *approximately* 50,000 rupees.
> He had *almost* reached the speed of 100 kmph when the car broke down.
> *Around* 70 protestors were arrested by the police.
> It is feared that *nearly* 125 people were drowned when the boat capsized.
> It takes *roughly* four hours to complete the task.
> *Some* 50 articles were published by her.

Arabic Words. See **Foreign Words and Phrases.**

As per for 'according to' or 'in accordance with' is very commonly used in India but is poor English and should be avoided in formal composition. As legalese it may perhaps pass muster. A sentence like this is inelegant:

> *As per* the new procedure, you have to produce your identity card before entering.

This sentence is better drafted thus:

> *According to* the new procedure, you have to . . .

Assonance is a figure of speech in which (1) the same vowels sound with different consonants in relative juxtaposition, or (2) different vowels sound between the same consonants, particularly used in verse.

> BCCI has now ruled 'no *pay* for no *play*' for those players who have to sit out in a match. [1]
> To *shift* the *shaft* from its original location is impossible. [1]
> She didn't invite me to her party and I won't invite her as *tit* for *tat*. [2]

All the summer through the *water saunter*. [2]

Assume; presume. *Assume* means 'to take upon oneself' and implies a justifiable motive, while *presume* means 'to take for granted' implying believed to be true but without proof.

> While investigating the case the police wrongly *assumed* that he was the thief.
> In Indian jurisprudence an accused is *presumed* to be innocent until proved guilty.

Asyndeton is a figure of speech in which conjunctions are omitted in a sentence:

> He came, he saw, he conquered.
> It is a printer, a copier, a scanner, a fax.

At, in, on. These three prepositions cause a lot of confusion. They act as function words.

Examples of correct usage are given below:

> She is still working *at* the problem.
> The party was held *at* his house.
> She is very good *at* badminton.
> He was called to the office *at* short notice.
> She is working *in* the kitchen.
> I solved the puzzle *in* no time.
> There were only 10 people *in* the hall.
> Swimming *in* the lake is prohibited.
> The soldier was wounded *in* the leg.
> The dinner is *on* the table.
> Be careful, he has a gun *on* him.
> The meeting will be held *on* the next Sunday
> He has a blister *on* his hand.

Aunt and **uncle** are not indicative of precise relationships. *Aunt* may be the sister of one's father or mother, the wife of one's father's brother, or one's mother's brother's wife. *Uncle* may be brother of one's father or mother, husband of one's father's sister, or husband of one's mother's sister. In Indian languages, there are different words for these different relationships. It is a common practice in India to address a senior or elderly person (even a stranger) as *Aunty* or *Uncle*, because in our culture people generally do not address such persons by name.

Average; mean; median. A layman is likely to confuse between the usage of these three mathematical terms. In an *average* or *arithmetic mean* the result is arrived at by dividing the total of a set of figures by the number of figures. [Geometric mean is different.] *Median* is the value that represents the point at which there are as many numbers above as there are below in a set of ordered numbers.

> The *average/mean* of $3 + 4 + 5 + 8 + 10 = 30 \quad 5 = 6$.
> The *median* of numbers 3, 4, 5, 8 and 10 = 5.

Bad; badly. Verbs of the senses—such as feel, look, smell, sound, taste—when used to express a condition rather than an action are connecting or linking words, and so their modifier must be an adjective and not an adverb
>I feel *bad*.
>>He looks *smart* in his new uniform.
>>The flowers smell *sweet*.
>>He sounds *terrible*.
>
>He was hurt *badly* after he fell from the roof.
>>He saluted the officer *smartly*.
>>She talked *sweetly* to the child.
>>She was *terribly* annoyed by his rude behaviour.

Bangalored is a newly-coined slang word by the Americans which refers to workers laid off because their jobs were relocated to India. The term takes its form from the Indian city of Bangalore which is the original hub of off-sourcing of jobs from the United States of America, Britain and some other countries.
>He was banglored because his job was outsourced to India

Basic point is 1/100th of a percent, a term that one often encounters in financial news in the daily newspaper.
>Bank interest has been reduced by 50 basic points.

Bear is a verb essentially meaning 'to endure' or 'to contain'; its past tense is **bore** and past participle is **borne;** also **bearing.** Verbal phrases formed from *bear* have different meanings.
>She is a brave woman and *bore* her loss with great fortitude.
>Some air-*borne* pollens cause allergies to humans.

bear down means 'to approach'.
>The storm *bore down* with such severity that all structures in its path were destroyed.

bear on means 'concern'.
>This order has a *bearing on* the admission process in the college.

bear out means 'to confirm'.
>When the ring was found in her bag it *bore out* the fact that she was the thief.

bear up means 'to endure'.
>She is *bearing up* under the strain of managing her family and the new job.

bear with means 'to put up with'.
> There was no alternative but to *bear with* the crass behaviour of her boss.

Because is as a conjunction and to start a sentence it is frowned upon by the purist. However, the modern usage permits it to be used as the starting word in a new sentence (like **And** and **But**).
> Because there was no electric power in the village she studied under a kerosene lamp.
> Because of crop failure several indebted farmers in Vidarbha committed suicide.

Because; since; as. As a conjunction *because* is more specific for expressing cause or reason, but *since* or *as* can replace it without changing the meaning in the following examples:
> *Because* the river was flooded it was difficult to reach the town.
> *Since* the river was…
> *As* the river was…

Since has also the connotation of time and no other word in this sense can replace it adequately:
> He has stayed in the house ever *since* his wife died.
> He has been out of a job ever *since* he graduated.

As is an adverb and a conjunction both:
> His farm boasts of many fruit trees such *as* mango, litchi, guava and banana.
> He is *as* cool *as* a cucumber.

Below; beneath; underneath. These three words have similar meanings but there are shades of difference. *Below* is at/on a lower level irrespective of amount of separation. *Beneath* is lying under a lower position directly under something. *Underneath* means lying directly under or beneath within something.
> The village lies in the valley *below* the hill.
> The flat *beneath* his is occupied by an old couple.
> *Beneath* his gruff manner lies a tender heart.
> Police commandos wear a bullet-proof vest *underneath* their uniform.

Beside; besides. The two words are interchangeable in some senses but not always. *Beside* means 'by the side of'. *Besides* means 'in addition to' or 'other than'; it also has the sense of 'moreover' and 'furthermore':
> She walked to the school *beside* me.
> He lives *bedside* my house.
> The argument is not relevant and *besides* the point.
> *Besides* paying her a fat salary he has provided her with a car.
> *Besides* five years in prison he was fined five thousand rupees.
> One should wear heavy clothing, *besides* strong boots while walking through the underbrush.

Between; among. There is a general impression that *between* can be used only in speaking of two persons or things, and *among* between more than two. This is not correct. It is perfectly correct to use *between* for more than two items when the number is unspecified.

> The two share the work *between* themselves.
> No agreement could be reached *between* the three warring parties.
> There should be no secrets *between* friends.
> It was decided to distribute the property equally *among* the four brothers.
> He is *among* the distinguished novelists who were given the award this year.

Bi- is a suffix which means 'two'. But it is rather confusing in its usage as it could mean either 'two times' or 'twice' in a given time period, particularly when used with a week, month or year. *Biweekly*, for example, could be used in both senses of 'twice in a week' or 'every two weeks'. It is better to use *fortnightly* in the sense of 'a period of two weeks'; and use *semi-weekly* for occurring 'twice in a week'. *Bimonthly* creates the same confusion and unless the sense could be made clear by a clue or in some other way it is best to be avoided. *Biannual* is used for 'occurring twice a year, and *biennial* for occurring every two years.

The use of bi- prefix in some other case does not cause any confusion, such as:

biaxial = having two axes
bicameral = having two legislative chambers
bicentennial = 200th anniversary
biconvex = convex on both sides
bifocal = as in glasses for distant and close vision.
bilateral = having two sides
bisexual = having characteristics of both sexes

Biannual; biennial; bimonthly; biweekly. These adjectives cause confusion because they may mean 'twice' or 'every two times'. There is no ambiguity between *biannual* which means 'twice in a year', and *biennial* which means 'once in two years'. But confusion arises with the use of prefix '-bi' which may mean 'two': either 'occurring two times' or 'occurring every two times'. This is especially true of *bimonthly* and *biweekly*, which when used without clarification puzzles the reader. To make the meaning clear it is therefore, advisable to use the prefix 'semi-' if you mean 'twice' (semi-monthly or semi-weekly), and 'every two months' or 'every two weeks' or fortnightly (twice in a month). Some other words with prefix 'bi-' are given in the examples.

> The journal of the society is a *biannual* publication. [comes out twice in a year]
> The carnival is held *biennially*. [every two years]
> The company issues its Newsletter *twice in a month / week*.
> The company issues its Newsletter *every two months / weeks*.

The *bilateral* agreement between the two parties was signed yesterday.
She uses *bifocal* glasses.

Biography and **hagiography** mean the same: written life of a person, but *hagiography* is particularly that of a saint. However, the current usage of *hagiography* refers to the biography of a person written in his or her idolising praise.

French's chronicle of V. S. Naipaul's life is in true sense a *biography* for it describes his life,
warts and all.

The recently published biography of the cinema star is not a true biography but a *hagiography,* treating her as a goddess and only eulogising her but glossing over all her blemishes.

Black of course is a colour and when used for a person (often capitalised) it indicates that they are of Afro-American origin. *Black* also signifies something negative when used in some phrases. *Black market* is illicit trade in officially controlled commodities. *Black magic* involves incantation for evil purposes. *Black mark* is a negative observation on a person's misdemeanor. *Black sheep* is a person of disgrace in a family or group.

Brackets are marks used in pairs to separate and enclose some matters from the surrounding material. Brackets are of four types: **(1)** *parentheses* or *round brackets*: they enclose a word or phrase in writing to indicate a thought or explanation in the form of a digression; examples abound in this book. **[2]** *square brackets*: they are used to clarify some point as seen at several places in this book; particularly used to enclose **[sic]**. {3} *braces* or *curly brackets*: mark to connect words or items considered together, and as mathematical notations; sometimes used singly to cover several listed items and lines. <4> *angle brackets:* used to enclose words or figures so as to separate them from their context in linguistics, technical and computer writing. [Note: in some European languages, these symbols are used as quote marks. In mathematics, < is the symbol for *less than*, and > is the symbol for *greater than*.]

Brands as generic terms. There are certain brand names which have become synonymous for their kind of products even if manufactured by other companies with other brand names. They have become generic terms for all products of the same kind in India; some are used in verbal forms.

Dalda = hydrogenated vegetable oil (ghee)
Formica/ Sunmica = plastic-treated laminated sheet
Hawaii chappal = rubber slippers (original a Bata brand)
Mobiloil = lubricating engine oil for vehicles
Vaseline = petroleum jelly

Brands as Verbs. Some brand names are now used as verbs because of the activity they represent.

Google = to search information from the internet, particularly from Google.com
> I *googled* to find information about the latest techniques of farming.

Hoover = to clean with a vacuum cleaner [from vacuum cleaner brand Hoover]
> She was *hoovering* the carpet when the bell rang.

Xerox = to photo-copy [from Xerox brand of photocopiers]
> I had the documents xeroxed for distribution.

Bravery and **bravado** are both words to describe 'courage'. However, bravery is the genuine act of courage, but bravado is—in a manner of speaking—contrived courage, either a swagger or a foolhardy conduct.
> Several soldiers showed real courage in fighting the enemy and earned *bravery* awards.
> In an act of foolish *bravado* a man tried to copy the stunt man and jumped from the running train, only to break his leg.

Break is a verb essentially meaning 'to suddenly divide or separate into parts'. Its past tense is **broke** and past participle is **broken**. Verbal phrases formed from *break* have different meanings.
> The *break* between them was complete when she returned the ring to him.
> The vase could *break* if handled carelessly.
> She *broke* her fast with orange juice.
> The temple *broke* the orthodox convention when a dalit was appointed its priest.
> His own previous record was *broken* when he hit two consecutive centuries.
> The vase was *broken* when it fell down from the shelf.

break away denotes 'to escape from something'.
> He decided to *break away* from the group.

break down means 'to cease to continue'.
> The talks between the union and management *broke down*.

break into means 'to force entry into a building'.
> Thieves *broke into* the flat after smashing the locks.

break off signifies 'to abruptly end or discontinue something'.
> The management decided to *break off* the talks after the union leaders became abusive.

break out means 'to emerge or erupt'.
> The epidemic of plague *broke out* in Surat due to unsanitary conditions in the city.

break up signifies 'to end a relationship or gathering'.
> The girl *broke up* with her fiancé after a quarrel.
> The meeting *broke up* after passing a vote of thanks to the outgoing president.

break with means 'to part with something'.
> She *broke with* the custom of arranged marriages and married the boy she loved.

Brethren is used sometimes as the plural of *brother* but this use is archaic. The proper use of *brethren* is for those who share with others common bond or interest, particularly of a religious order.

> Indian Muslims are very concerned about the treatment of their *brethren* in Iraq.

Bring is a verb essentially meaning 'to fetch'. Its past tense and past participle is **brought**. Verbal phrases formed from *bring* have different meanings.

> A new canal has been built to *bring* water to the parched land.
> The government is to *bring* a new legislation on reservations.
> Police *brought* the prisoner to court in a closed van.
> The fire alarm *brought* everybody running out of the building.

bring about means 'to cause':
> His love of the bottle *brought about* his downfall.

bring down means 'to fall down':
> The effort of the government to *bring down* the prices has failed

bring forth means 'to produce' or 'generate':
> The government is to bring forth a legislation to regularise the slums.

bring in means 'to introduce':
> The judge *brought in* a verdict of guilty.

bring off means 'to succeed in':
> He *brought off* the deal by offering an unmatchable amount.

bring on means 'to cause something to happen':
> He *brought on* the trouble on himself by his own actions.

bring out means 'to produce something':
> The company is *bringing out* a new magazine by January next.

bring round means 'to restore to consciousness':
> It was very difficult to *bring round* the staff to work on Sunday.

bring up means 'to raise something':
> She is likely to *bring up* the matter of rising prices in Parliament.

But is a conjunction to link two sentences or phrases and according to purists it should be in the same lengthy sentence. However, it is longer frowned upon to start a new sentence with *But*.

> After the storm the house was badly damaged and required extensive repairs. *But* it is safe to live there now.

Can; could. *Could* is the past tense of *can*. *Can* suggests the ability to do something', while *could* implies a 'condition'.

> You *can* come and stay with me.
> He *could* come and stay with me if he brought his own bedding.
> She is so nimble that she *can* climb the tree in a jiffy.
> She *could* play the harmonium with both hands.

Can; may. *Can* implies 'be able to', and *may* indicates 'possibility or probability'. In several cases *can* and *may* are interchangeable.

> He *can* come and stay with me. [the offer is positive]
> He *may* come and stay with me. [the offer is tentative]

It may be noted that only can and may have the possibility of being constricted in the negative:

> He *can't* come and stay with me.
> He *mayn't* be the most suitable boy.

Cannot is contraction of 'can not', and its current usage as one word is considered proper. Its contraction is *can't*.

Capitalisation. Numerous words are written with the initial letter always in capital.
  1. First word in a sentence and line of poem
  2. Pronoun 'I'
  3. Personal names and proper nouns, along with titles, if any.
  4. Names of organisations, public and government
  5. Place and geographical names
  6. Heavenly bodies
  7. Peoples and languages
  8. Months and weekdays; and holidays
  9. Names of religions and religious books
  10. Names of deities
  11. Titles of books, literary works, newspapers, magazines, journals, etc.
  12. Names of ships and aircraft.

Capitalisation of Celestial Bodies. The names of all celestial bodies are always captalised, but 'sun', 'earth' and 'moon' are also written without capitalization as commonly used words. The word *earth* is not capitalised in general writing when it is used in the meaning of 'soil' or 'the ground'; or 'the world we live in'. It should otherwise be capitalized in the sense of a planet—just like the 'Venus' and the 'Mars', for example—especially in scientific writing it should always be capitalised: the *'Earth'*. Similarly, the 'moon' as a common object may not be capitalised but when used in the sense of a satellite or in astronomical and scientific writing it should always be capitalized. This also holds true of the 'sun', which as a common object is not capitalized, but in scientific writing it needs to be capitalised: the 'Sun' (because it is a star). The 'sun' is also used as a synonym of a star as a celestial body. All names of celestial bodies are preceded by 'the'.

> A little *earth* was taken by each mourner and thrown into the grave.
> The potter took a little *earth* and created an exquisite bowl from it.
> Geology is one of the *earth* sciences.
> Among the planets, *Earth* is third from the *Sun*.
> Sedimentary rocks cover nearly three-fourths of the exposed *Earth's* surface.
> Fossils are used to build the evolutionary life on the *Earth*.
> The *Earth* wobbled very slightly during the Sumatra earthquake of 26th December 2004.
> The *moon*-lit night bathed the whole landscape with a magical luminescence.
> One complete *Moon* cycle consists of four phases.
> The *Earth* has only one natural satellite, the *Moon*.
> The *Sun* is the centre of the solar system.
> There are so many other *suns* in our galaxy.

Capitalisation of Geographical Names. Both the parts of the name of a geographic feature are capitalized, but when writing together the names of two or more features the rank of the feature is in lower case. The names are generally preceded by *the*.

> Himalaya Mountains [But: Himalayan peaks]
> Aravalli Range
> Western Ghats
> Nilgiri Hills [But: Nilgiri and Cardamom hills]
> Mount (Mt.) Everest
> Ganga River/River Ganga [But; Ganga and Godavari rivers]
> Pacific Ocean [But: Pacific and Atlantic oceans]
> Arabian Sea
> Bay of Bengal
> Hudson Bay
> Persian Gulf
> Gulf of Mexico

Dal Lake
Lake Superior
Kashmir Valley
Valley of Flowers

Carat; karat. *Carat* is the unit of weight of precious stones equal to 200 milligrams (1/5th of one gram). Karat is the unit of fineness of gold, where pure gold is 24 karats making it 1/24th part of pure gold in an alloy.

> The famous Kohinoor diamond weighs 105.60 *carats.*
> Her bangles are made of 22 *karat* gold.

Cardinal numbers. A cardinal number denotes quantity (one, two, three, and so on) that is used in simple counting, and can be written in numerals or words. It is opposed to an ordinal number (first, second, third, and so on) [See **Numeral expressions**)

Chair commonly is understood as a piece of furniture having four legs and a back for seating a person. It is considered here in the meaning of 'a professorship' and 'a person presiding over a meeting, conference, etc.' The latter is a shortening of *chairman, chairwoman,* and *chairperson*. It is also a verb to mean 'preside'.

> He holds the university *chair* of Ancient History and Culture.
> She is the *chair* of the first session of the symposium.
> We have asked her to *chair* the meeting.

Chiasmus is a figure of speech or rhetorical construction in which there is an inverted relationship between the second phrase or clause of the order of words from the first. It is a very effective way to hammer home a point.

> There is no way to peace—peace is the way. (Mahatma Gandhi)
> Ask not what your country can do for you, but what you can do for your country. (J.F. Kennedy)
> Let us never negotiate out of fear, but let us never fear to negotiate (J.F. Kennedy)
> Some people eat to live, others live to eat.
> We don't know what we don't know.
> The more things change the more they remain the same.
> Some things are good from far, but far from good.

Chinese words. Several words from various Chinese languages have crept into English, some through trade and some from the culinary route, but they are not many. Due to the popularity of Chinese food names of dishes like *chow-mein, dim-sum, chop suey,* etc., are now house-hold words. So are *ketchup* and *tofu*. Some generally-used words are given here with their meaning. These words are generally not italicized.

chow = any type of food
> I am starving and let's have some *chow* now.

gung ho = enthusiastic and eager participation in an activity.

C

> She had practiced long and was *gung ho* about participating in the tournament.

honcho = big shot; boss
> He is the top *honcho* of the IT company.

kow-tow = to show deference
> A large number of people *kow-tow* to him now that he has become a minister

mandarin = a high ranking officer or bureaucrat
> The *mandarins* of the Home Ministry have decided not to deploy the rapid-action force there.

yen = craving; strong desire
> The *yen* to eat ice-cream was very strong though she is a diabetic.

Clause is a group of words being a distinct part of a compound or complex sentence including a subject and predicate; it usually contains a verb and may or may not be a sentence in its own right. Care should be taken in writing a sentence with multiple clauses to avoid any confusion. In the following examples the clauses are shown separated by a slash and the conjunction is underlined. [Compare with **Phrase**]

> "He has a rough exterior / <u>but</u> a soft heart"
> This is a new book / <u>which</u> everyone wants to read.
> He won the scholarship / <u>for</u> which he had worked hard.

Cliché is defined as a trite, hackneyed or commonplace phrase, expression or idea. But which phrase or expression is a *cliché* may be a matter of opinion. Commonly used expressions considered by some as a *cliché* may actually be a phrase appropriate to the occasion and may convey the meaning what he rightly wants to use for effect. Some times such a phrase of a few words conveys the exact sentiments which would otherwise require many words to explain the thought. Some clichés are respectable idioms.

> I will *leave no stone unturned* to ravel this mystery. [try every possible means]
> He is *second to none* in patriotism. [surpassed by no one]
> *In this day and age* [now-a-days, nowadays]
> The food is *to die for*. [extremely good or desirable]
> I will *cross the bridge when I come to it*.
> What has been done cannot be helped, there is *no use crying over spilt milk*.
> The president of the society *was conspicuous by his absence*.

The following *clichés* are polite expressions to avoid making a blunt statement of death:

> His father *departed for his heavenly abode* on Sunday.
> Her brother *passed away* last Tuesday.
> The office mourned the *sad demise* of the Manager.
> He has instituted a medal in honour of his *dear departed* father.

Climate; weather; season. *Climate* is the general weather conditions prevailing over an area or region extended over a long period of time. *Weather* is the day-to-day atmospheric conditions of temperature rain, wind, etc., for a certain time and place. *Season* is each of the four common division of the year—spring, summer, autumn, and winter—marked by particular weather patterns and daylight hours; there could also be other seasons consisting of a particular period of the year, like 'rainy season', mango season, mating season, etc. The first two terms often cause confusion and care should be taken to make the necessary distinction.

> The *climate* of India is tropical with three distinct *seasons* of winter, summer and monsoon.
> The best time to plant rice is the rainy *season*.
> In the mango *season* the market is flooded with several varieties of the luscious fruit.
> The *weather* during our trip to Manali was atrocious, it rained all the time and when it cleared we were lashed by strong, chilling winds.

Clippings. See **Contractions of Noun.**

Collective nouns are group terms that are singular but take a singular or plural verb depending on the meaning to be conveyed.

> The *government* fell when *it* lost its majority.
> The *government are* responsible for all decisions taken by ministers.
> The *committee is* scheduled to meet on Friday.
> The *committee* of three *are* expected to inspect the site today.
> The *army was* deployed in the troubled North-East.
> The *army are* responsible for the safety of the nation.
> The school *has* a dedicated *staff* of highly qualified teachers.
> The *staff are* encouraged to develop a warm relationship with the kids.
> A *group* of people *is* resisting the move.
> A *group* of disgruntled people *are* resisting the move.

Colloquialism. It is informal language that is more common in conversation than in formal speech or writing. Of course, it is permissible in writing to quote verbatim what is actually said.

Come is a verb having the meaning of 'draw near', arrive at', 'happen' and so on. Its past tense is **came** and past participle is **come.** Verbal phrases formed from *come* have different meanings.

> I have *come* here after summons from the boss.
> The time has now *come* for some plain speaking to the staff.
> She *came* running when I called her.
> The apples *came* from Himachal Pradesh.
> Her prediction *came* true when the book hit the best-seller charts.
> *Coming* to think of it you have done a really good job.

come about means 'to happen' or 'to occur'.

> It so *came about* that both were in school together.

come across has the meaning of 'to discover' or 'to find'.
: She *came across* as a reliable witness.

come along conveys the meaning of 'to accompany'.
: He asked me *to come along* with him on the trip to Manali.

come apart means 'to break'.
: The book was so old that it *came apart* as soon as I opened it.

come around has the meaning of 'to accede' or 'to yield'.
: He came *around* to my view after I briefed him with the facts of the case.

come between means 'to interfere'.
: Her father *came between* the two to resolve the dispute.

come by means 'to acquire'.
: A good job is hard to *come by*.

come down means 'to descend'.
: The heirloom has *come down* to me from several generations.
: The police has *come down* heavily on the drug mafia in the city.

come in means 'to arrive'.
: She *came in* just in time for the dinner.

come off conveys the meaning 'to happen' or 'to occur'.
: It appears that he will *come off* lightly from his misadventure.

come out means 'to result'.
: After interrogation it *came out* that he was the culprit.

come round means 'to accede' or 'to yield'.
: After a lot of discussion the manager *came round* to his views.

come through has the meaning of 'to accomplish' or 'to survive'.
: In the interview he *came through* as well-versed in the subject.
: He *came through* the ordeal without any harm.

Compare. There is a difference between *compare to* and *compare with*. *Compare to* signifies 'to liken one thing to another'; *compare with* indicates 'to note resemblance or difference between two things or persons'.
: As *compared to* a buffalo, a cow gives less milk.
: He is much more gentle as *compared to* Shyam.
: *Compared with* the national average his income is not bad.
: You can't *compare* his achievements *with* those of Shyam.

Comrade simply means a 'companion', but in public perception he is a communist or fellow traveller and the word is also used to address such a person.
: *Comrade* Jyoti Basu was the Chief Minister of West Bengal for almost two decades.
: The *comrades* have laid siege in a West Bengal village called Nandigram.

Compass directions in a sentence are generally written in lower case but capitalized in certain cases [see **North** and **South**]. *South India* and *the North-East* [India] are capitalized. The style of writing other directions of the compass is as follows:

northeast – north-northeast
northwest – north-northwest
southeast – south-southeast
southwest – south -southwest

Competent; efficient; proficient.. These three adjectives qualify the abilities of a person but have different shades of meaning: *Competent* means 'having the ability or qualification required by the work in hand'; *efficient* means 'working productively for desired effect without waste'; and *proficient* means 'skilled or adept'.

> She is *competent* to teach mathematics as she has a PhD in the subject.
> He is very *efficient* as any task given to him is carried out without delay.
> She is very *proficient* in French and has been employed by UN as an interpreter. .

Compounder is a word not found in any English dictionary though the word has been in wide use and well-entrenched in India for over a century, introduced possibly in mid-nineteenth century, to designate a person in a physician's clinic who fills prescriptions, dispenses medicines, gives injections, dresses wounds, and carries out other medical duties. Perhaps this name was given in the early days to the person who 'compounded' several drugs to prepare a mixture (medicine) to fill a physician's prescription—much before the advent of packaged medicines. Although numerous Indian words have been absorbed in the English language this word has not been accepted so far by the lexicographer. This term is so well entrenched and so widely used in India that it deserves a place in the English lexicon along with numerous words that have been absorbed from India.

Comprise. The word means 'to include' or 'to be made up of'. *Comprises* has the meaning of 'inclusive of' and to use the phrase 'comprises of' is incorrect, but is widely used. However, the expression 'comprised of' is correct in sentence formation. Another correct usage is when the verb is in the gerund form. Care should be taken for the correct and proper use of *comprise*.

> The kit *comprises* a note book, two pencils and a rubber eraser. [Correct]
> The kit *comprises of* a notebook, two pencils and a rubber eraser. [Wrong]
> The *kit is comprised of* a note book, two pencils and a rubber eraser. [Correct]
> A kit *comprising* a notebook, two pencils and a rubber eraser is available to students. [Correct]
> The task force *comprises* people from several disciplines. [Correct]
> The task force *comprises of* people from several discipline. [Wrong]
> The task force is *comprised of* people from different disciplines. [Correct]

The task force *comprising* people from several disciplines was formed in 1988. [Correct]

The seven states that *comprise* the North-eastern Council have separate budgets. [Correct]

The seven states that *comprise of* the North-eastern Council have separate budgets. [Wrong]

The seven states that are *comprised of* the North-eastern Council have separate budgets. [Correct]

There are seven states *comprising* the North-eastern Council [Correct]

Computerspeak. Computers have developed their own lingo and it is interesting to note that many common words and expressions are ordinary ones but given new meanings after capturing by the geeks. It is amusing to note several such.

bit is not a piece of anything, *but* is a *b*inary dig*it*, a measure of the capacity of a microprocessor.

boot is not what you wear on a foot, *but* the word for starting a computer and readying it for operation.

bug is not an insect, *but* a problem that prevents a computer programme from working properly.

bus is not a vehicle to take you places, *but* a set of parallel conductors in a computing system that forms the main transmission path.

chip is not a small piece of wood, *but* the brain of a computer.

cookie is not a biscuit for you to nibble on, *but* an application's ability to work interactively with a user, remembering all data stored in the computer.

hard drive is not a long, grueling journey, *but* is the part for storing massive amounts of information on the computer.

hardware is not what you bought from an ironmonger's shop, *but* the physical parts of computers and associated devices.

log-on is not to add wood to a fire, *but* to start or access a programme on the computer.

mouse is not a small rodent, *but* a pointing devise to provide input for the computer that practically controls all the computer functions.

spider is not a repulsive insect, *but* a person or a software programme that searches for links on the Web.

Trojan-horse was intended to undermine something, *but* is a hidden programme that breaches the security of a computer.

virus is not a pathogen that makes people ill, *but* a nasty programme code that damages computer files and data.

Windows are not openings in a wall for looking out, *but* an operating system of the computer.

Web is not a network of fine threads constructed by a spider, *but* a comprehensive information system on the Internet.

worm is not an invertebrate creeping animal, *but* a self-replicating nasty programme in the computer similar to a virus.

Computer terminology. The computer has created its own jargon which mints new terms and redefines old words at such a fast pace that make you dizzy. Such words may be called 'computerese'. These are besides those noted above.

blog. A website that is a kind of personal diary in which all kinds of personal information, including pictures and videos, is posted. [from we*b-log*]

Bluetooth. Wireless network connection to exchange information between devises, such as between mobile phone, laptop, digital cameras, etc.

FaceBook. A social networking website that connects people with friends and others who work, study and live around them.

Firewall. A computer safety system to prevent network intrusion

geek. Overtly intellectual person, particularly expert in computers.

hacking. Breaking into other people's computer and modifying a programme illegally.

nerd. An obsessive computer person.

Netizan. A person who frequently uses the worldwide Internet for information.

Orkut. A social networking website sponsored by Google that allows you to post personal or professional information and links to friends and acquaintances.

phishing. A technique to gain personal information for purpose of identity theft, using fraudulent e-mail messages.

spam. Unsolicited bulk e-mail.

wardriving. Breaking into unsecured wireless internet.

wilfing is surfing the Net aimlessly.

YouTube is a video-sharing website whose users can upload, view and share video clips.

Conjunctions. *As*, *because*, *for*, and *since* are used as conjunctions to link two clauses.

In the following sentence *as* can be replaced by *because*, *for*, or *since* without changing the meaning:

The doctor advised him rest *as* he was overworked.

Contraction of nouns (also called **Clipping**) is shortening by deleting a part of the word. This is not abbreviation and no stop is used within a sentence. Some examples:

ad = *Ad*vertisement

bra = *bra*ssiere
bus = omni*bus*
cycle = bi*cycle*
exam = *exam*ination
flu = in*flu*enza
gym = *gym*nasium
lab = *lab*oratory
Memo = M*emo*randum
phone = Tele*phone*
photo = *photo*graph
plane = Aero*plane* / Air*plane*
pub = *pub*lic house

Contraction of verb phrases is shortening by insertion of an apostrophe in place of the omitted vowel or syllable in writing, and in pronouncing. These contractions are to be avoided as far as possible in ordinary written prose unless they form part of a conversation piece or dialogue. In the following examples the omission or elision is indicated by an apostrophe. [see also **Elision**]

can't = cannot
don't = do not
doesn't = does not
hasn't = has not
haven't = have not
I'd = I had; I would
I'm = I am
It's = it is; it has
let's = let us
we're = we are
won't = would not

Contraction of year date. It is advisable to write the year in full in a date, but in diminutive form the first two numerals could be and generally are omitted with the use of an apostrophe. But in a complete date the apostrophe is generally omitted in its diminutive form. Examples:

The year 1989 could be contracted to '89 [But: 22-06-89 or 22/6/89]
The year 2005 could be contracted to '05 [But 22/6/05]

Continual; continuous. There is fine distinction in the meaning of the two words. *Continual* relates only to time and applies to something that 'keeps of recurring' or 'goes on incessantly'. *Continual* implies a close prolonged succession of an event. And continuous refers to 'uninterrupted action in time and space'. Sometimes both words may be used as synonyms.

Floods keep occurring continually in the Brahmaputra Valley
There were *continual* showers throughout the day. [with short interruptions]
The ocean is in *continual* motion.

Steel making is a *continuous* process [uninterrupted]
The *continuous* whirr of the machines is very jarring.

Cost as a verb has its past tense and past participle as the same **cost**, but in some cases **costed** can be used in the past tense often with **out (costed out)** to estimate or set the cost of a thing or procedure, but otherwise it should be avoided.
> The *cost* of living has gone high after the increase of petroleum prices.
> The long absence from work *cost* him his job [Not: *costed*]
> The house *costed* him a lot of money. [Correct: *cost*]
> It will *cost* a lot to get my damaged car repaired.
> The company *costed out* the retiring benefits of its employees. [Correct]

Council and **Counsel** have quite different meanings. *Council* [noun] is an administrative or deliberative body, but *counsel* is 'a lawyer' as noun and 'to advice' as verb.
> The Uttar Pradesh *Council* has decided to honour its past chairmen by having their portraits displayed in the foyer. [Noun]
> The Executive *Council* of Lucknow University has introduced several new courses this year. [Noun]
> She has employed a new *counsel* to represent her case before the court. [Noun]
> She was *counseled* to avoid any hasty action in the matter. [Verb]

Couple and **pair.** Both these words though singular refer to two entities combined, and generally take a singular verb. However, in certain constructions where the two parts are concerned separately they take the plural verb as the following examples would show:
> A couple *lives* in the second-floor flat who *have* separate bedrooms.
> The pair *is* employed in the same company but they *work* in separate departments

Cousin is an English word indicating relationships which confuses an Indian as it doesn't give a clue whether the relative is male or female and the degree of relationship. It generally means 'a child (male or female) of one's uncle or aunt (*first cousin*)', but also takes care of several other relationships unlike in an Indian language. A cousin may be relative descended from one's grand parents or more remote ancestors by two or more steps and in a different line. Different degrees of relatives are indicated by using such expressions as 'first cousin twice removed', 'second cousin', 'second cousin once removed', and so on. Indians used to the concept of an extended family are often baffled as many such relationships have special terms.

Credible and **credulous** are both adjectives referring to 'belief'. *Credible* means 'which is believable', while *credulous* refers to a person who is 'too ready to believe even on slight evidence'.

There is *credible* evidence that the theft was carried out by the Banjara gang.
She is so *credulous* that she believed the cock-and-bull story spun by the servant.

Cricket lingo are some cricketing expressions that have become a part of the ordinary language, especially in cricket-playing nations such as India. Some examples:

bowled over = completely overwhelmed or surprised
: He was *bowled over* by her beauty the very first time he met her.

clean bowled = thoroughly impressed
: She was so smart that the interview board was *clean bowled* by her answers.

duck = zero
: He played well in the first inning but in the second he was bowled for a *duck*.

hit for a six = completely defeated
: Her scheme was *hit for a six* when the committee refused to support her.

off one's own bat = through one's own effort
: No body helped him and his success was achieved by playing *off his own bat*.

play a straight bat = give a non-committal answer
: He is a smart politician and *played a straight bat* during the press conference.

send down a bouncer = pose a difficult question
: For all his bravado he was nonplussed when a correspondent *sent down a bouncer*.

send down a googly = pose a difficult question
: The Foreign Office spokesman was fielding all questions with aplomb but clammed up when a correspondent sent *him a googly* about scam in an embassy abroad.

sledging = offensive remark
: It is not only cricket *sledging* happens in other sports as well.

sticky wicket = in a tight situation
: He got into a *sticky wicket* when he could not produce the accounts.

stumped = nonplussed
: He thought he was smart but was *stumped* by a question the examiner asked him.

tail-ender = placed at the bottom
: She is a sweet little girl but a *tail-ender* in the class.

Criterion and criteria. Though *criteria* is plural of *criterion* it is often wrongly used as singular. The correct usage of the two is:
: The *criteria* for the job are very stringent.
: The single *criterion* for appointment to the post is a good typing -speed.

Customer; client; patient. Customer is a general term for one who purchases a commodity or service from a shop or business establishment. (The word is also used for person having a specific tribute, such as 'a real tough customer'). Lawyers have 'clients', and doctors have 'patients'.

Cut is a verb which essentially means 'divide'. Its past and past participle is the same **cut**. Verbal phrases formed from *cut* have different shades of meanings.

cut away means 'to chop off'.
> They had to *cut away* a portion of the carpet to fit the room.

cut back means 'to reduce or shorten'.
> To *cut back* expenses the company has decided to abolish free mid-day meal to the staff.

cut down means 'to reduce'.
> To reduce expenses the company decided to *cut down* some allowances of the staff.

cut in means 'to interrupt'.
> She *cut in* their conversation to announce that it was time to go.

cut off means 'to disconnect or discontinue'.
> Their scholarships were *cut off* when they failed to pass the examination.

cut out means 'to exclude'.
> In her will she *cut out* her son who never bothered about her.

cut up means 'to divide'.
> The whole property was *cut up* in four parts, one for each child.

Dashes. Among the punctuation marks in printing, dashes are of two types: *Em-dash* is the width occupied by M and in printing there is no space between it and the preceding and following letters—like this, while the *N-dash* is half of em-dash and there are spaces on both sides – like this. A pair of dashes is used to enclose any small and distinctive material that is included in a sentence without structurally essential to it just like a pair of commas or round brackets. Dashes are not preceded or followed by commas, but at the end of an exclamation or query mark one may be put if required. A single dash is used to indicate the source or quotation.

> The local people—otherwise peace-loving—gave the chain-snatcher a good beating before handing him over to the police.
> The local people – otherwise peace-loving – gave the chain-snatcher a good beating before handing him over to the police.
> The two brothers—they aren't known exactly to be gentlemen!—surprised everyone by taking the injured child to the hospital.
> The resident association has decided to hire private guards—isn't it the responsibility of the police?—for security.

Data is the plural of the singular 'datum', and requires a plural verb. However, it is commonly used as singular with a singular verb. Though this is not correct, *data* is often considered a mass noun which takes a singular verb.

> The census *data shows* that there are more males in the village.
> The experimental *data show* that this is not possible.
> [Also] The experimental *data shows* that this is nor possible.

Dates can be written in several forms. The logical way is to write a date in this order: day→month→year. However, the ever popular style now is to follow the American style: month→day→year. In India, confusion occurs when the American style is abbreviated, such as 9/11/02 where one does not know whether it is the 9th November or the 11th September. Incidentally, this date is now famous as the day on which terrorists demolished the twin towers of the World Trade Center in New York City.

> January 24, 2008 [1/24/08]
> 24 January, 2008 [24/1/08]
> 24th January, 2008 [It is desirable to add 'the' before the date written in this style in a sentence]

Definite; definitive. These two adjectives do not convey exactly the same meaning. Definite means 'not vague or ambiguous', while definitive has the sense of 'something authoritative'.

It is now *definite* that he will take over as the director.

A *definitive* biography of Indira Gandhi is now being written.

Demi-; Semi-; Hemi-. All the three prefixes mean 'half', but the usage is different. *Demi-* is used with words of French origin; *semi-* with words of Latin origin; and *hemi-* for words of Greek origin.

> demigod; demimonde; demipension
> semi-annual; semicircle; semifinal; semi-liquid; semiprecious
> hemisphere; hemicycle; hemihedral

Deprecate; depreciate. The verb *deprecate* means 'to express disapproval of", while *depreciate* indicates 'diminish in value of a thing over a period of time' or 'to disparage, belittle or lower the esteem of something'.

> She *deprecated* the attitude of several parliamentarians who kept postponing the consideration of the Women's Bill under one pretext or the other
> The value of Rupee has *depreciated* over a period of time.

Desperate and **disparate** are similar looking adjectives but have different meanings. *Desperate* is an adjective meaning 'extremely bad or serious involving or employing extreme measures'. *Disparate* has the meaning of 'essentially different'.

> He was *desperate* to get to America and bribed the agent ten lacs.
> There was *desperate* shortage of food during the infamous Bengal famine.
> The two things are as *disparate* as chalk and cheese.
> The two have disparate philosophies: one believes in violence and the other puts its faith in peaceful negotiations to achieve their objective.

Despite; in spite of. Both mean the same and can be used interchangeably, though *in spite of* seems more emphatic. Note that *in spite* is two words and not one, and is followed by 'of'.

> *In spite of* the rain the function was held in the open.
> *Despite* the rain the function was held in the open.

Diacritical marks are signs used to indicate different phonetic values in spelling words incorporated in English vocabulary from some other European languages, particularly French. For instance, the Standard English word *resume* (verb; pronounced: *rizum*) means 'to begin again', but with diacritics the French-origin *résumé* (noun; pronounced: *rezumey*) means 'summary' and is used in the sense of 'curriculum vitae'. The following are the main diacritical marks and their names; sounds and accents.

′ Acute accent (Orléans; blasé, névé, résumé, cliché)

°	bolle (nostrum units) [Swedish language]
˘	Breve (Brĕton, brĕvet) [used to indicate a short vowel or short or unstressed syllable]
¸	Cedilla (façade; française) [mark under c to show that it is a hissing sound]
˜	Circumflex (château) [mark placed over vowels to indicate accent]
`	Grave accent (crèche, après) [mark placed over a vowel to indicate altered sound]
¯	Macron (bāzār) [placed over a vowel to indicate that the vowel is long]
ʹ	Soft sign (Akhangel'sk)
·	Superior dot (sharzysko kamienna]
~	Tilde (cañon, señor, São Paulo) [mark placed over letter to produce sound *ny* or nasal]
¨	Umlaut or dieresis (Nüremberg, Brontë, naïve) [mark placed over a vowel to indicate a more central articulation

Diphthong is a union of two vowels pronounced as a single vowel in one syllable, with or without a ligature. **Ligature** is a printed or written character consisting of two or more words joined together, such as Æ, æ, Œ, and œ. Some European languages use such ligatured letters but these characters are being abandoned, mainly because of typing problems, and the two characters A + E, a + e and O + E, o + e are typed separately. The spelling, again, has been further rationalized in many cases—particularly in American spelling—by getting rid of the ligature and also the vowels 'a' and 'o' as their sounds are almost mute. In the examples given below these changes are clearly illustrated:

encyclopædia   encyclopaedia   encyclopedia
palæontology   palaeontology   paleontology

There are certain words where the original ligature has disappeared but both the vowels are retained in pronunciation though the first is somewhat mute.

Ægean Sea   Aegean Sea
Æsop fables   Aesop fables
Œdipus complex   Oedipus complex
onomatopœia   onomatopoeia

There are other words in which 'a' and 'e' or 'o' and 'e' come together, but not as ligatures. A + e and o + e sound nearer to 'e' and modern spellings omit the 'a' and 'o' without much affecting the pronunciation.

aesthetics   esthetics
oedema   edema

oesophagus	esophagus
oestrogen	estrogen
Palaeocene	Paleocene
Palaeozoic	Paleozoic

In certain Greek words, vowels are still written with a ligature, as in Ægean Sea and Æesop, but for practical purposes the two vowels are written without the ligature in English.

There are several words where vowels 'a' and 'e' come together, and 'e' tends to be half mute:

aeroplane
aerosol
aerial

Direct; directly. The adjective *direct* is used for 'straight' and *directly* is often used wrongly for in the same sense. But the correct meaning of *directly* is 'without delay' or 'at once'.

> He went *direct* to his office from the station. [Straight]
> This is a *direct* train to Delhi. [Straight]
> We will be home *directly* after the show. [Immediately]
> Hearing the news I went *directly* to the hospital. [Without delay]

Discreet; discrete. These two adjectives are often confused in usage. *Discreet* means 'cautious in speech or action', while *discrete* has the meaning of 'separate' or 'distinct'.

> He was *discreet* and refused to be drawn into the controversy.
> River and lake are two *discrete* bodies of water and require different kinds of treatment.

Disinterested; uninterested. The two words have a subtle difference in their meaning. While *disinterested* conveys a sense of impartially that a person is 'not personally interested or concerned', *uninterested* conveys 'general lack of interest'. An old joke illustrates it the best:

> The *disinterested* judge listens to arguments from both the sides, but the *uninterested* judge falls asleep during the arguments by the lawyers.

Distinct; distinctive. Of the two adjectives, *distinct* is something readily distinguishable by the senses as 'something different from others', while *distinctive* denotes that it has 'some individual characteristic and is distinct from others'.

> *Ram Charit Manas* of Tulsidas and *Valmaki's Ramayana* are two *distinct* versions of the same epic *Ramayana*.

Characters of the twins, Seema and Sheela, are very *distinct*: Seema is an athlete interested in outdoor activities, while Sheela is a bookworm hardly getting out of her house after school.

The *distinctive* feature of the Caspian Sea is the high concentration of salts in its waters so that it is practically impossible to drown.

The African elephant is recognized by its *distinctive* large ears.

Drama and **play** are two words related to acting (performing a role in a play or film). *Drama* is a genre of literary style intended to tell a story by action and dialogue on stage, film or anywhere else. (It also means a series of exciting or emotional incidents and events and may not be connected to a literary event.) *Play* in this context is the literary form of a story that can actually be performed on stage, radio or television.

> A *drama* festival is being held in Delhi in which troupes from several countries are taking part.
> There was a great *drama* when the police went to arrest Indira Gandhi after she lost the election.
> Shakespeare's *play* The Merchant of Venice has been prescribed as a textbook for Class XII.

Due to; owing to. There is subtle difference between the two phrases. *Due to* has the meaning of 'caused by', and that of owing to means 'because of'. But in effect both the phrases are often interchangeable. It may be mentioned here that once the phrase *due to* was frowned upon because 'due' is an adjective and should not be used as a prepositional phrase, but its use has become so common that it is now accepted as standard English. *Owing to* was preferred but it is also a prepositional phrase and as valid as *due to*. Often *due to* sounds better than *owing to* at the beginning of a sentence.

> The road to Shimla was closed *due to / owing to* heavy snowfall.
> The company suffered a huge loss *due / owing to* his negligence.
> *Due to* unavoidable circumstances the programme was cancelled.

Duplicate and **replicate** as verbs, the two have the same meaning of 'to make exact copies of'. *Duplicate* means to 'produce exactly the same thing again'. *Replicate* has the sense of 'repeating the same'.

> The notice was *duplicated* and copies displayed at various places in the campus
> The cold fusion experiment could not be *replicated* at any other laboratory.

Dutch words. Several words from the Dutch language are commonly used in English writing. Here are a few [See also **Afrikaans words**]

booze = drink to excess
boss = master; overseer
cookie = a sweet biscuit
cruise = sail about for pleasure

dam = barrier to hold back water from a stream
furlough = leave of absence
landscape = inland scenery
mart = market
quack = a medical charlatan
skipper = captain of a boat or team of players

Dysphemism is a figure of speech in which an offensive word or expression is used in place of one that is neutral or normal and is meant to disparage or offend.

> Do you think that your bird-brained son can ever get a good job?
> Ha! He wants to sell the pile of junk which he calls his car.
> He has delusions of grandeur for he still behaves as a maharaja though his privy purse was abolished long back.
> He pretends that he is a great author though his desk is littered with rejection slips

Each; every. *Each* means 'being one of two or more individuals or things'. *Every* has the meaning of 'entire body of people or things'. Both the words are sometimes interchangeable.

Each and *every* one of us is responsible to the society.
Each one of us is to plant a sapling in her garden.
Every one is expected to plant a sapling in one's garden
Each player was given a chance to bat.
Every player was given a chance to bat.

Each other; one another. The two expressions are to be applied in different situations but are very often used indiscriminately. To avoid confusion, it must be remembered that *each other* applies to 'two persons or things', but *one another* to three or more.

They hit each other indicates that only 'two persons' were involved, but *they hit one another* clearly shows that three or more persons were involved.

Eastward; eastwards; easterly; eastern. The writer gets perplexed by the correct use of the first two words. *Eastward* is adjective and adverb both, meaning 'in an easterly direction' and *eastwards* is adverb only meaning 'towards the east'. Since the sense is the same, either can be used. *Easterly* has the meaning of 'in an eastward position or direction' or 'coming from the east' particularly with reference to wind. Eastern means 'coming from the east', referring specially to the regions to the east of Europe.

The *eastward*-facing windows get the first morning sun.
If you look *eastwards* you can see the ruins in the distance.
The *easterly* winds sweep into Alwar a lot of sand from the Thar Desert.
Among the *Eastern* nations China is now the most developed.

Either. The word (i) means 'one or the other', or (ii) is used for emphasis.

You can take *either* road to reach the town.
How can I employ her? She is not educated or smart *either*

Either / neither; any. *Either/ neither* should only be used with reference to two things, but if there are more than two *any* is the appropriate word.

Either Ramesh or Umesh can go and fetch the car.
Neither Ramesh nor Umesh know driving.
Any person, who has a licence, could take the car to the station.

Either/ or; neither/ nor. *Either* acts as a function word before two or more coordinate words, phrase or classes joined by *or* to indicate that what follows immediately is the first of the two or more alternatives. The first in each pair follows the second in sentences involving unavoidable choice between two or more alternatives.

>The way he is behaving it looks he is *either* drunk *or* mad.
>*Either* you can join the army, *or* you can continue with college.
>The nurses in this hospital are *neither* competent *nor* caring.
>She is always asking for some thing; it is *either* a new sari, *or* a new ring, *or* a new pair of chappals.

Elder, elderly, and **older** in respect to human relationship have different connotations. *Elder* is a person of greater age than one. *Elderly* is rather an old or aging person, past middle age. *Older* is a comparative of 'old'.

>He is my *elder* brother.
>He is an *elderly* person.
>This sister is *older* to me by three year

Elision is suppression of vowel or syllable in pronouncing. See **Contractions of verb phrases.** Some other examples are given here:

>goin' = going
>there's = there is

Ellipses are three dots indicating omission of words in a quoted passage or a pause in writing; at the end of a sentence it indicates trailing off in an intriguing or fascinating manner something unsaid.

>The output of the printed word in the English language . . . is simply phenomenal.
>The fight got out of hand; he threatened: "If you don't go away at once I am going to . . ."

Emigrate; immigrate. The meaning of *emigrate* is 'to go to live permanently in another country.' It is just the opposite of *immigrate* which means 'come to settle permanently in another country'.

>He plans to *emigrate* to Australia soon.
>Karl *immigrated* to India from Germany.

Endemic; epidemic; pandemic. These three similar words cause some confusion when describing the prevalence of diseases. *Endemic* means that the disease is restricted to a particular region or people. *Epidemic* occurs when an infectious disease is suddenly affecting a large population or area. *Pandemic* indicates that the disease is affecting a wide geographic area like a whole country or a large part of the world and population.

>Malaria is *endemic* to the terai region of Uttar Pradesh.
>The plague *epidemic* in Surat devastated the whole town.

> There is a danger that the foot-and-mouth disease if not controlled immediately may become a *pandemic*.

Endemic is also used in the sense of prevalence or characteristic of a restricted area or occurrence other than a disease.
> This variety of mango is *endemic* to Malihabad near Lucknow.
> The problem of giving sustainable wages to the weavers of Varanasi is *endemic*.

Enquiry and **inquiry** are both nouns that mean the same, but there is a fine shade in the meaning of the two. *Enquiry* connotes 'a request for information (used often in the plural), while *inquiry* has now come to indicate 'a regular investigation into a matter of public interest'.
> He made *enquiries* about the day train to Delhi.
> The *inquiry* commission was given another extension of six months.

Epanalepsis is a figure of speech in which there is repetition of a word or a phrase in a text or speech as a rhetorical device. The following quotation from the war-time speech of Winston Churchill is the finest example of epanalepsis ever.
> We shall fight on the beaches, we shall fight on the landing grounds, we shall fight in the fieldsand in the streets, we shall fight in the hills, we shall never surrender.

Epigram is a short and pointed, terse or witty saying or expression, often paradoxical, effective by its wit and ingenuity. It requires considerable flair to write epigrammatic language. The following couplet by poet Samuel Coleridge' definition of this form is in itself an epigram:
> What is an epigram? A dwarfish whole:
> Its body brevity, and wit its soul.

Another well-known example of epigram comes from Alexander Pope:
> A man who knows the price of everything but the value of nothing.

Epigraph is a short quotation or saying at the beginning of an article, chapter or book intended to suggest its topic or theme. This device could be used by a writer to introduce a reader to the topic or to lay emphasis on what he intends to say. (It is also an ancient engraved inscription by a ruler or other authority.)

Epitaph is an inscription on a tomb in memory of the person buried there, as also words written in memory of a deceased person.

Epithet is an adjective expressing quality or attribute of a person or thing or it may be offensive or abusive word or phrase. [not to be confused with **epitaph**.]
> *Jholawala* is an epithet that is applied to an Indian pseudo-intellectual who moves around with a cloth shoulder-bag containing a few Marxist books and sprouting platitudes.
> He calls himself a painter but his work is no better than a *child's doodle*.
> He thinks he is clever but I think he is only a fool and *bird-brained*.
> When he tried to teach me morality, I got annoyed and told him *to go to hell*.

Esquire (abbreviation **Esq.**). It is elegant to use the title *Esq.* after the name of a gentleman. A comma is used after the name and before *Esq.* If this title is used, *Mr.* is omitted, that is, both Mr. and Esq. cannot be used at the same time.

> H. M. Malhotra, Esq.
> Mr. H. M. Malhotra
> [*Not*: Mr. H. M. Malhotra, Esq.]

Etc. is the abbreviation of Latin *et cetera* meaning 'and the rest'. It is generally written after an incomplete list of two or more things or persons to indicate that there are additional unspecified items in the list. Therefore, to write 'and' before the last item in the list is meaningless because it indicates finality to the list. Another abbreviation of this phrase is **&c.** but it is avoided in a sentence. A comma is used before *etc.*, and sometimes also after it in American usage.

> You must bring pen, pencil, scale, *etc.*, for the examination.

Euphuism is a figure of speech where an offensive, harsh or distressing expression is substituted by one which is gentler though may be less accurate. This original definition has been extended to include all words and expressions without any such connotation. Such forms are popularly used in everyday writing or speech because they are often mild, decent and polite expressions.

> *better-half* = wife
> *collateral damage* = unintended killing of civilians in war
> *domestic help* = servant
> *flesh trade* = prostitution
> *mentally deranged* = mad
> *passed away* = died
> *shrink* = psychiatrist
> *sanitary convenience* = lavatory
> *senior citizen* = old man

Another type of euphuism can be considered a **sobriquet**:

> *The Bard* for 'Shakespeare'
> *The Mahatma* for 'Mahatma Gandhi'.
> *The Raj* for the British sovereignty in India

Some words or phrases could be considered euphuism:

> *fancy wheels* [fancy cars]
> *the stork came calling* [a child was born]
> *open the bubbly* [celebrate by opening Champaign]

Even date, of. Of the same genre as *instant*, *ultimo*, etc., this expression is very confusing in letters and memos. It means 'today', and is a good example of muddled writing, for one has to look up the date without which it makes no sense. (God save you if you happen to read the memo on a later date.)

> With reference to your memo of even date I confirm the venue of the meeting.

Fall is a verb which means 'to descend freely' or 'to drop down'. Its past tense is **fell** and past participle is **fallen.** Phrases formed from *fall* have different meanings.

>His *fall* from grace was complete when the pink slip was handed over to him.
>Her *fall* was broken by the overhanging branch of a tree.
>Darkness *falls* rather early during winters.
>The dress *fell* gracefully from her shoulders.
>He has *fallen* in esteem of his colleagues.

fall apart means 'to break' or 'to disintegrate'.
>His life *fell apart* after the death of his father.

fall back has the meaning of 'to retreat' or 'to have recourse to'.
>The intruders *fell back* after the fierce attack by the paramilitary forces.
>The unit *fell back* on the emergency rations when fresh supplies failed to reach it.

fall down has the meaning of 'to descend'.
>He *fell down* from the tree but escaped with only bruised shins.

fall for has the meaning of 'to fall in love' or 'to be deceived'.
>She *fell for* the dashing soldier.
>He *fell for* the ruse and parted with ten thousand rupees.

fall in means 'to take ones place', or 'to collapse'.
>He *fell in* line after he was threatened with dismissal.
>The roof of his house *fell in* after the earthquake.

fall in with has the meaning of 'to agree', 'to comply', or 'to support'.
>She *fell in with* the views of the other jurors and agreed to acquit the prisoner.

fall into means 'to get into'.
>He started gambling as he *fell into* bad company.

fall off means 'to drop down'.
>He *fell off* the cliff when his legs slipped.

fall on/upon means 'to attack fiercely or unexpectedly'.
>The crowds *fell upon* the thieves and beat them mercilessly.

fall out means 'to quarrel' or 'to disagree'.
>The lovers *fell out* and broke the engagement.

fall through means 'to come to nothing'.
>The proposal to build a new culvert *fell through* because of paucity of funds.

fall to means 'to start'.
> He *fell to* the task with renewed zeal after appreciation from the supervisor.

Family relationships. Brother and sister are biological offspring of the same parents. But the qualifiers 'half-' and 'step-' cause much confusion in describing other siblings.

Half-brother/half-sister is related through one biological parent only, which means that one has only one biological parent in common. A *stepbrother/ stepsister* is a son/daughter of one's step-parent by a marriage other than that with one's own biological father or mother. *Stepson/Stepdaughter* is a son/daughter of one's husband or wife by a previous marriage. *Stepfather* is a man who is married to one's biological mother after the divorce of one's parents or the death of one's biological father. *Stepmother* is a woman who is married to one's biological father after the divorce of one's parents or the death of ones biological mother.

Farther and **further** are two words that are often used interchangeably as comparative of 'far' in the sense of 'greater distance', but now there is a subtle difference in meaning between the two. *Farther* is now used in the meaning of 'additional distance' *Further* has the meaning of 'additional'
> I got no *farther* than my door when it started raining.
> He lives a mile *farther* than my house.
> Nothing could be *farther* from the truth.
> The school will be closed until *further* notice.
> It will take *further* ten minutes to reach his house.
> He took *further* training to qualify as a test pilot.

Fatal; lethal. Both the adjectives refer to 'something ending in death' but there is a clear distinction: *fatal* means 'resulting in death' (as also 'completely destructive or ruinous'), while *lethal* means 'causing or designed to cause death'. It is absurd to say that "He had a *fatal* accident but survived." If an accident caused death, how can any one survive later?
> The accident was *fatal* and he died instantaneously.
> The decision to open his shop during riots proved *fatal* as it was burned down completely by the rioters.
> *Lethal* chemicals were leaked by the plant and several people died.
> In some countries death sentences are carried out by a *lethal* injection.

Few; a few; the few. In some cases, the absence or presence of an article or modifier changes the meaning of some words. Two words that are commonly affected and are widely misused are *few* and *little*. *Few* means 'a small number' or 'not many', and *little* means a small 'quantity or degree'. Used alone these two words have the connotation of 'not many' or 'not much'. *A few* means 'a small number' or 'some at least' and *a little* means 'a small amount of' against 'many' or 'large'. Few is very often used in Indian writing when the writer actually means to convey 'a small number'. [See also **Little**]

> *Few* people could attend the meeting because of the rains. [Small in number, not many]
> He is a man of *few* words. [Only some]
> *A few* shops were open during the riots. [A very small number]
> *The few* shops that open on Sundays sell only groceries. [Select minority]
> *The few* friends he had deserted him after his conviction. [Select minority]

There are other expressions, like *a good few* and *quite a few*, which mean 'a fairly large' or 'considerable number'.

> Although it was snowing hard, *a good few* of his friends were present at his wedding.
> *Quite a few* mourners were present at the funeral though it was snowing.

But *very few* denotes 'a really small number'.

> There are really *very few* people who want to join the scheme.

Fiancé and **fiancée** are two very similar nouns related in meanings that are often confused. *Fiancé* is a man engaged to be married, while *fiancée* is a woman engaged to be married. In other words, the man is known as the woman's *fiancé*, while the woman who is engaged is known as the man's *fiancée*.

> Radha is going to be married to her *fiancé* Sunil on the 12th June.
> Sunil's wedding with his *fiancée* Radha is fixed for the 12th June.

Figures of speech are styles or expressions that add attractiveness, charm and interest to any writing and speech. Even scientific or business reports laced with figurative language add to the pleasure of reading a dry subject. They should be used appropriately to enhance reading pleasure. There are several kinds of figures of speech, and they are discussed at appropriate places in this book. A good writer effortlessly uses the various figures of speech possibly without being able to identify it with the appropriate nomenclature.

Final; finale. The adjective *final* means 'the last' or 'decisive', and another adjective *finale* formed from it has the meaning of 'the closing part of a public event like an opera, drama, music, etc.'

> The *final* cost of the project will run into 2000 crores.
> The *final* solution of the problem is to close the office.
> There was an impressive march past of the medalists at the *finale* of the games.

Find; find out (and the past and past participle **Found**). Sometimes it is confusing to decide whether one or the other of the two is appropriate to use in a particular context. *Find* mans a simple 'search' or 'discovery'. *Find out* has an element of effort involved in it. The following examples will elucidate the difference.

> I will *find* time to search for it
> I *found* time to search for it.

The boss *found out* that the search was a sham.
I *find* that milk is rich in calcium.
Enough calcium is *found* in buffalo milk.
I *find* that the milk has gone bad.
I *found out* later that the milk was adulterated
I *find* that there is no solution to the problem.
I *found* a solution to the problem.
I *found out* later that the problem has already been solved.

First is an ordinal number that comes before all others in time or order. Used in a phrase it has different shades of meaning.

first aid = emergency care or treatment
After the accident, the victims were given *first aid* before the ambulance arrived.

first class = high quality
Everything sold in our store is *first class*.

at first = at the beginning
I thought *at first* that it was a fire cracker but it was a bomb.

first and foremost = more important than anything else.
The *first and foremost* requirement for the employee is his knowledge of book-keeping.

first and last = on the whole
The manager I employ must be honest, *first and last*.

first of all = most importantly
First of all the integrity of the cashier should be without reproach.

first thing = before anything else
The *first thing* you should do on reaching Kolkata is to call on the manager

in the first place = as the first consideration
In the first place, I require a house with a garden.

of the first order = excellent
The cuisine offered by the restaurant is *of the first order*.

first hand = direct personal experience
She had *first hand* knowledge of office procedure because for long she was secretary to the managing director.

first rate = excellent
She is *first-rate* badminton player.

First World = highly developed and industrialised nations
G-8 is a group of *first world* leaders.

Flavour and **fragrance** are words which refer to physical sensation but are sometimes confused in usage. *Flavour* refers to taste in the mouth only and its use to describe a smell is archaic at best and should be avoided. *Fragrance* refers to a pleasant or sweet odour or smell.

> This talcum powder has the *flavour* of the rose. [Wrong]
> This talcum powder has the *fragrance* of the rose {Correct]
> The *flavours* of langra and Dussehri mangos are quite different.
> The *fragrance* given by the chameli flowers at night is overpowering.
> The scents of this brand are available in a variety of *fragrances.*

Foreign Words and Phrases. One of the reasons of wide-spread acceptance and popularity of English is its capacity to embrace words from other languages. The influence of European languages, both modern and classical, is natural; it was supplanted by infusion from languages of its erstwhile far-flung global empire and other tongues. The result is that the English language has been enormously enriched by acceptance and absorption of foreign words, some have been so assimilated that they have become indistinguishable parts of its vocabulary. Words like *alcohol, algebra, alkali, almanac, cipher, magazine*—believe it or not—are just modified Arabic words. Such foreign words and phrases (sometimes from their derived meaning) are very useful in conveying and expressing thoughts (and things) more cogently and appropriately. A selection of foreign words and phrases from some chosen languages in general use in English writing are listed under appropriate headings.

Former; latter. It is quite common to find *former* and *latter* being used when referring to two things in the same text mentioned earlier. The reader finds it cumbersome and annoying to refer back to what has been said before in a long text. It is better to mention again the matter concerned. The only concession to use these two words could be to avoid repetition of the original if the sentence is not too long and if the matter may sound stilted if the concerned words are repeated again and again.

> There has been a lot of speculation whether the Prime Minister will give him the Finance or the External Affairs portfolio. It is informally gathered that he would prefer the *former* and the *latter* going to another minister. [This is a short text and former and latter can easily be comprehended but in a long text there could be confusion.]

Fractions in words. Writing fractions, such as, and , in words is sometimes confusing. In the first four examples below, one is only a single part of one-third and one-fourth and so the singular is used. In the remaining, it is two-times one-third, three-times one-fourth, five-times one-eighth and so its plural form is required though, the verb remains singular. The simple rule is that if the fractionated number is more than one it requires a plural. All fractions less than '1' (one) use a singular verb.

The insect was only *one-half* inch long.
One-third of the district is prone to floods.
One-fourth of the property went to charity.
One quarter of the property went to charity.
Two-thirds majority is required to pass an amendment. [Not: *two-third*]
Three-fourths of the land is cultivated. [Not: *three-fourth*]
Three -quarters of the land is cultivated.

Frantic and **frenetic** are two adjectives meaning exactly the same 'widely excited with fear, anxiety etc.' Apparently, the usage may be considered a personal choice, but it may be noted that *frenetic* is more often used in America.

Free; freely. The adjective *free* means 'without charge' or 'at liberty'. The adverb *freely* made from it means 'without restraint'.

The government has arranged for *free* meals in schools.
Feel free to use my car whenever you want.
A mixer-grinder is given *free* with the refrigerator.
The government has been elected *freely* by the people.
The governor mingled *freely* amongst the people.

French words and phrases. A large number of French words and phrase are in common use in English prose. The earlier practice was to italicise them but in current usage italicisation is increasingly being avoided and they are being printed in the normal Roman type. It may be noted that the diacritical marks are retained in both italic and normal types. A list of such words and phrases in general use is given below:

au revoir = good-bye till we meet again
avant garde = leaders or pioneers in new and unconventional movement in art
belles letters = purely literary writing; sophisticate literature
bete noir = particularly disliked person or thing
café = a small restaurant for light meals and drinks
cause célèbre = lawsuit that attracts much attention; a notorious episode, incident, or thing
cliché = a hackneyed theme or expression
cul-de-sac = passage, street, etc., closed at one end)
déjà vu = illusory feeling of something familiar
de luxe = of superior kind, luxurious
de rigueur = required by custom or etiquette
enfant terrible = person causing embarrassment by unruliness
en masse = all together, in a body or as a whole
en route = on the way
faux pas = a social blunder; a tactless act; breach of good manners

femme fatale = dangerously attractive woman
force majeure = unforeseeable course of events
haute couture = high-class and fashionable dress-maker's products
hors-d'oeuvre = appetizer extra dish
joie de vivre = feeling of healthy and exuberant enjoyment of life
nblesse oblige = obligation of honourable generous and responsible behaviour
nom de plume = pseudonym of a writer
nouveau riche = one who has newly acquired wealth
par excellence = greatest degree of excellence
passé = out-of-date
raison d'etre = purpose or reason to justify a thing's existence
résumé = summary: in the meaning of curriculum vitae
vis-à-vis = in relation to

Function Words are those words (preposition, conjunctions, or auxiliary verb, etc.) which have no intrinsic meaning but contribute to the essential grammatical meaning to a phrase or sentence.

German words. Several words of German origin have come into use, particularly after the two World Wars. They are not italicized in English writing.

blitz = Intensive, sudden course or action

blitzkrieg = Intensive military campaign intended to bring about a swift victory

frankfurter = A seasoned sausage made of beef or pork

hamburger = A round patty made up of a bread roll filled with meat or other fillings

kaput = Broken and useless

kindergarten = A school or class for very young children

kitsch = Garish, tasteless art or design
> Calendars generally print pictures of gods and goddesses which are nothing but *kitsch* art.

leitmotiv/leitmotif = a dominant recurring theme in a composition

Gerund is a verb that ends in '-ing' and works as a noun describing action or process.
> *Working* as the manager, he was able to maximize profit of the company.
> No *smoking* is allowed in the office.

Get is a verb which has several meanings of 'to earn', 'to catch', 'to seize' and so on. Its past tense and past participles is **got.** Verbal phrases formed from *get* have different meanings.
> She *gets* nothing from the court after the divorce.
> I *got* to the airport after the flight had left.
> She *got* talking to her neighbour in the morning

get across means 'to communicate' or 'to convey'.
> He *got across* his ideas of progress by a power point presentation

get ahead means 'to advance' or 'to progress'.
> He *got ahead* in his career by dint of hard work.

get along means 'to cope' or 'to progress'.
> She is a friendly soul and *gets along* well with all her colleagues.

get around means 'to circumvent'.
> She *got around* the problem simply by buying a new dress.

get at means 'to reach' or 'to find out'.
> She *got at* the problem at once and took corrective measures.

get away means 'to escape'.
>The prisoner *got away* from jail by scaling the outer wall.

get back means 'to recover' or 'to take revenge'.
>She *got back* her hard earned money after several months.
>She *got back* at her tormenter by filing a counter claim.

get by means 'to cope' or 'to survive'.
>After her husband's death she *got by* working as a domestic help.

get down to means 'to give serious attention'.
>He *got down* to the point as soon as the meeting started.

get in means 'to enter'.
>He kept shouting and she couldn't *get in* even a word in explanation.

get off means 'to move' or 'to separate'.
>He *got off* lightly only with a fine.

get out means 'to escape'.
>He could *get out* only after paying a hefty fine.

get out of means 'to avoid'
>He could not *get out of* the mess despite all efforts.

get over means 'to surmount' or 'to convey'.
>She could *get over* the trauma of her son's death after long psychological counselling.
>She could not *get over* her point of view to the new manager.

get round 'to circumvent' or 'to persuade'.
>To *get round* the legal hurdle it was decided to change the land-use.
>She *got* him *round* to her point of view with some difficulty.

get through means 'to reach the end of something difficult'.
>She could *get through* the examination with some difficulty.

get together means 'to assemble'.
>They all *got together* to pay for a new ping-pong table.

get up means 'to arise'.
>He *got up* in the morning with high fever

Glossary is a kind of dictionary of a specific subject in which words with explanation are arranged in alphabetical order. Academicians or scientific writing in their particular field would do well to consult a *glossary* of that subject.

Give is a verb with several meanings like 'to bestow', 'to execute', 'to yield', 'to produce', etc. Its past tense is **gave** and past participles is **given.** Verbal phrases formed from *give* have different connotations.
>The organisation *gave* blankets to the poor last winter.
>The court has *given* permission to the builder to construct a mall on the land.

The new wheel chair *gives* her confidence to feely move about the house.
She *gave* birth to a bonny little boy.
The children have *given* a fine performance in the school play.
The farm *gives* three crops a year.

give away means 'to reveal' or 'to make a present'
Under pressure from police he *gave away* the place where the arms were hidden.
She *gave away* her inheritance to charity.

give in means 'to submit or yield'
After persistent questioning the prisoner *gave in* and admitted his guilt.

give off means 'to discharge or emit'
After heating, the material *gives off* a foul smell.

give out means 'to distribute'
The postal department has *given out* a new uniform to its employees.

give up 'to relinquish or surrender'
The family has *given up* their struggle to regain their property.

Go (also **goes** and **going**) is a verb with several meanings, essentially 'walk' or 'move'. Its past tense is **went** and past participle is **gone**. Verbal phrases formed from *go* have different meanings.

I advised him to *go* slow in the matter.
She *went* to Delhi by train.
She *went* to sleep late at night.
These clothes *go* to the top shelf in the wardrobe.

go about means 'to perform' or 'to undertake'.
She *went about* her business as if nothing had happened.

go after means 'to seek' or 'to get'
She *went after* her tormenter determined to teach him a lesson.

go against means 'to defy'.
She *went against* the family's wishes and married her boy friend.

go ahead means 'to advance'.
She *went ahead* with her plan to open a school for underprivileged children.

go along with means 'to express agreement'.
She decided to *go along* with the majority and voted for the motion.

go at means 'to set about'.
She decided to have a *go at* cracking CAT.

go away means 'retreat' or 'vanish'.
She thought that by swallowing an aspirin her headache will *go away*.

go back means 'retract'.
He *went back* on his word to give her a job.

go by means 'to lapse'.
: As the time *goes by* his gout gets worse.

go down means 'to fall' or 'to collapse'.
: He *went down* fighting the enemy though he was mortally injured.

go for means 'to choose' or 'to attack'.
: She *went for* an MBA degree because it would further her career.
: The shikari *went for* the tiger that had turned a man-eater.

go in for means 'to choose' or 'to take part in'.
: She likes to *go in for* commerce as a subject as it has better job prospects.

go into means 'to peruse' or 'to enquire'.
: He decided to *go into* the business of retailing.
: She *went into* all the details of the case before appearing in court.

go off means 'to happen', or 'to explode'.
: She *went off* in search of her lost pet dog.
: The bomb *went off* even as the police were searching the premises.

go on means 'to continue' or 'to persist'.
: She *went on* to take a degree in law and practice in the High Court.

go out means 'to leave' or 'to depart'.
: She *went out* in the evening to attend a party.

go over means 'to examine' or 'to peruse'.
: She *went over* the document to ensure that it was properly drafted.

go through means 'to examine' or 'to undergo'.
: She *went through* the document to ensure tat it was properly drafted.
: He *went through* a tough time fending off the eve-teaser.

go together means 'to agree'.
: The two don't *go together* in their views on birth-control.

go under means 'to fall'.
: She *went under* the spell of a man who posed as a guru.

go with means 'to agree'.
: The majority of members decided to *go with* the president to endorse the resolution.

go without means 'to do without:'
: She *went without* her breakfast as it was not ready.

Gobbledygook. An American coinage, the word means 'pompous, wordy and generally unintelligible jargon' which is often used in government and professional writing; it is an enemy of good and cogent style. Gobbledygook is to be avoided at all costs—and this book is there to help you. One example should suffice:

> In response to your esteemed letter of the 24th ult. requesting examination and comments regarding our proposal to prevent people from throwing garbage on the said road, I beg to say that instructions have been issued to the health authorities vide memo of the 5th inst. to do the needful.

Shorn of gobbledygook, this letter could be written as follows:

> Referring to your letter of the 24th May about throwing garbage on the road, the health authorities were instructed on the 5th June to prevent it.

Goods is the plural form of good, and in this form has an entirely different meaning of 'merchandise' or 'possessions'. The problem arises whether a single piece of merchandise could be referred to as singular 'good'? This appears absurd and for practical reasons *goods* could be used both in the singular and in the plural.

Graceful, gracious. *Graceful* is a physical attribute of a person meaning 'full of charm, courtesy and elegance'. *Gracious* denotes 'courteous and kindly consideration'.

> In his wedding finery the groom looked very *graceful*.
> Though in her fifties she still looks very *graceful*.
> She has the reputation of being a *gracious* hostess.
> She was *gracious* enough to pardon his mistake.

Grand and **Great relatives.** The relationships beyond the immediate family is qualified by prefixing 'grand' or 'great'. There can only be *grandfather, grandmother, grandson* or *granddaughter*. But the rest of relatives are qualified by 'great': *great-uncle, great-nephew, great-grandfather, great-granddaughter*, and so on.

Grammar is the study of the classes of words and their form, structure and functions (morphology) and their interrelations in the sentences (syntax). In other words, grammar is the organizing principle in which words are coined together suitably in a sentence to make sense of what is spoken or written. Though a writer may not remember or know the exact parsing of a word which he learnt in school, the knowledge of grammar in forming words into meaningful sentences is essential as without it what one wants to convey in writing and speaking would become gibberish and absurd. The generally recognized **Parts of Speech** (word classes) are the following: *noun* (name of peoples, places, things); *pronoun* (word in place of a noun); *adjective* (modifier of a noun); *verb* (describing action); *adverb* (modifier of a verb, adjective or other adverb); *preposition* (word governing a noun or pronoun); *conjunction* (word used to connect clauses); and *interjection* (exclamation).

Greek words. There are hundreds of English words that are derived from Greek after minor modifications in spelling. However, some are used without any change, such as aroma, aura, cell, dogma, drama, enigma, idea, mania, phobia, stigma, and so on. A few Greek phrases too make an appearance.

Green is, of course the name of a colour. But in recent years it has also been used in the sense of something which is environment-friendly or is concerned with or supporting protection of the environment. To *make anything green* has come to mean 'to make it less harmful to the environment'.

> CNG (compressed natural gas) is a *green* fuel for vehicles as it is less polluting.
> Cycling is a *green* and healthy way to live happily because it is non-polluting.
> The *green* movement is in favour of drastically reducing the use of plastic in everyday life as it is practically indestructible.

Grey is also the name of a colour but it has some other connotations as well. *Grey* denotes something that is vague in position, condition or character, such as a *grey market* which is one that is irregular and not accounted for officially or legally.

> The abortion law in India is not specific on certain matters and there is a *grey* area which is liable to be exploited by unscrupulous doctors.
> There is a large *grey market* in mobile phones where hand-sets are sold without the mandatory identification number.

Guarantee (guaranty); warranty. *Guarantee* is a written or other undertaking to answer for performance of some obligation. It is somewhat wider in implication than *warranty* which generally refers to a guarantee of the quality, performance, etc., of goods. The two words are often used as synonyms.

Hapless and **helpless** are both in reference to people in unfortunate circumstances. *Hapless* means 'unlucky' or 'unfortunate', while *helpless* indicates 'no defense or support'.

The *hapless* people in Castro's Cuba have to put up with all kinds of shortages.

The people were *helpless* when the Bhuj earthquake destroyed their homes.

Hard; hardly. The noun *hard* means 'strong' or 'that which does not yield easily'. The adverb *hardly* has the entirely different meaning of 'scarcely' and is not derived from 'hard' which is also the adverb of itself. Always remember the distinction between the two words otherwise you may land yourself in trouble!

> He worked *hard* to remove the debris. [strongly]
> His *hard* work paid and he was promoted. [tough]
> He worked *hardly* to remove the debris. [scarcely]
> I had *hardly* gone a few kilometers when the car engine failed. [scarcely]

He/ she; him/ her. A nominative pronoun goes as the subject of the verb, and an objective pronoun as object of the verb.

A man is *he* who can face the challenge of the mountains.

It was *she* we were talking about.

They invited *him* to participate in the event.

It is really nice of *her* to take part in the play

Hebrew Words. This is the language in which most of the Bible was written. These words have been in the English lexicon for a long time and are not italicised.

behemoth = Something of monstrous size or power

> ArcelorMittal is a *behemoth* ready to swallow small steel-makers.

cabal = A group engaged in a plot or intrigues

> A *cabal* of Janta Party parliamentarians have decided to block this legislation.

jubilee = A celebration of anniversary

> The golden *jubilee* of Indian Independence was celebrated with great fervour in 1997.

kosher = Genuine and legitimate. (Derived from food prepared according to Jewish laws.)

> Muslims eat only 'halal' meat as it is considered *kosher* in Islam.

messiah = An accepted leader of some hope or cause.
> Jaiprakash Narain was a *messiah* of the poor and the downtrodden.

methuselah = Very, very old person (Derived from Biblical character Methuselah who was reputed to be 999 years old.)
> He is quite a *Methuselah* but is ready to take part in the marathon.

sabbath = Seventh day of rest; a time for rest.
> For Jews and Christians Sunday is the day of *Sabbath*.

Height, elevation and altitude essentially mean the same but there are subtle differences in their use. *Height* is a general word for 'the distance from the bottom to the top of something standing upright'. *Altitude* is 'vertical height above a given level or reference point' such as the sea-level; it is also used in the sense for the 'angular elevation of celestial objects above the horizon' *Elevation* is almost a synonym for altitude, but is also used to describe 'the particular side of a building'.
> The *height* of this building is 52 metres.
> The recalculated *height* of Mt. Everest is 8850 metres above the mean sea level.
> The *altitude/elevation* of Mt. Kilimanjaro at 5895 metres makes it the highest point in Africa.
> The first Indian satellite will orbit the Earth at an *altitude/elevation* of 360 km.
> The eastern *elevation* of my new house gets the first rays of the rising sun.

Here and derivatives. This adverb gives rise to several other adverbs with different meanings.

hereafter means 'later; in the future' or 'after death'.
> *Hereafter* every one will clean his/her room in the morning.
> I believe in living life fully while I am alive, what happens *hereafter* I don't bother.

hereby denotes 'by this means'.
> I *hereby* declare that I leave all my property to the orphanage.

herein means 'in this thing'.
> *Herein* lies the remains of Josef Stalin.

hereto means 'in this writing or document'.
> I declare *hereto* that my son will be my successor as the chairman.

herewith means along this communication' or 'object'..
> I send *herewith* the required documents.

Heteronym is one of two or more words spelled alike but different in sound and meaning. There are not many such words, and the following readily come to mind:

<u>Bow</u>
pron. *bau* = to submit/yield/bend head or body in respect [verb]

pron. *bo* = a weapon made of wood or metal with a cord connecting two ends [noun]

Buffet
pron. *buffet* = to strike repeatedly and violently with great force [verb]
pron. *bufey* ('t' silent) = multi-dish meal where guests serve themselves [noun]

Live
pron. *liv* = to remain alive or have life [verb]
pron. *laiv* = that is alive or real or active [adjective]

Minute
pron. *minit* = one-sixtieth of an hour [noun]
pron. *mainiute* = very small [adjective]

Read
pron. *reed* = to reproduce mentally or vocally written or printed word [verb]
pron. *red* = past tense of the above

Row
pron. *rau* = to propel boat with oars [verb]; disturbance [noun]
pron. *ro* = more or less straight alignment of objects [noun]

Wind
pron. *vind* = natural movement of air [noun]
pron. *wyind* = to go in spiral or curved course [verb]

Hinglish is a word or expression coined to convey the use of a mixture of Hindi (or any other Indian language) and English that is frequently encountered among the English-educated classes in India. It is quite common in conversation to use an English word while talking in Hindi (or any other Indian language). Converse is also true: talking in English some words and phrases often creep in. Such mixed-word sentences are called *chutnification*—the word itself is a mixture formed by combining *Chutney* (Hindi)+fication (English suffix). This type of hybridisation is to be avoided in serious prose. Several English words have also penetrated the rural areas and it is not uncommon to hear them spoken by even unlettered rustics, maybe in a somewhat distorted or modified form. Even an unlettered rustic child more often than not addresses its parents as 'Mummy' and 'Papa'. Real chutnification occurs when the Hindi suffix 'ji' is added to form Mummy*ji*, Papa*ji*, Uncle*ji* and Aunty*ji*—which is quite common. Several hybrid expressions in the following examples were started by early

European settlers and the process is continuing. [See also **Indianism, Pidgin English**]

lathi-charge = beating of a crowd by the police.
chicken-tikka. = barbecued chicken
filmi = melodramatic action or situation
have a dekko = Have a look at something
press-walla = a guy who does ironing of clothes.
rickshaw-puller = a puller of rickshaw

Advertising and Hindi film titles have embraced Hinglish with great gusto.

Yeh dil mangta more [Ad slogan]
Hungry *kya*? [Ad slogan]
Jab We Met [Film]
Bheja Fry [Film]
Saas Bahu and Sensex [Film]

Hinglish titles. Numerous entities bear titles that are composite of Indian and English words. It is evident that the concerned English word has been appropriated and absorbed into Hindi. Even the government resorts to this type of hybridisation.

Bharatiya Kisan Union
Bhavishya Nirman Bond
Janta Party
Panchyat Raj Department
Rajdhani Express
Rozgar Guarantee Scheme
Sangeet-Natak Academy
Sasta Kirana Store

Historical dates. B.C. in historical dates is written after the year(s), the older date first and then the later date, because the older figure is earlier in time than the younger. In giving the A.D. dates it is the other way round as A.D. is written before the dates and not after in the following styles. To separate the dates an en-dash (–) is used rather than a hyphen (-).

325 B.C
325–220 B.C.
325 to 220 B.C.
A.D. 79
A.D. 1585–1627
A.D. 1585 to 1627

However, A.D. can be written after mentioning the century:

By the second century A.D. Christianity had spread to West Asia.

Hold is a verb to mean 'to grasp', 'to possess', 'to contain', 'to restrain', 'to think', and so on. Its past and past participle is **held**. Verbal phrases formed from *hold* have different meanings.

The child *held* her hand tightly in the crowd.
He *holds* properties in several towns.
The container *holds* five litres of petrol.
The police *held* the thief at gunpoint so it couldn't escape.
The priest *holds* strong views about abortion.
She *holds* a degree in business administration.

hold back means 'to restrain'.
She could not *hold back* her tears after hearing his story.

hold forth means 'to speak at length'.
The speaker *held forth* for such a long time that the audience became restive.

hold off means 'to avoid, or 'to delay'.
The police *held off* any action against him because he was an influential politician.
For the time being the action against him has been *held off*.

hold out means 'to offer' or 'to persevere'.
The company *held out* an offer that he could not refuse.
The dacoits *held out* until their ammunition was exhausted.

hold up means 'to support' or 'to delay'.
The government is *holding up* the price line by subsidies.
The government is *holding up* the reforms in view of the coming elections.

Homograph is a word spelled the same but meaning differently, for example *project* is both noun and verb with different meanings: Some authorities consider *homograph* equivalent to **Homonym**.

Homonyms are two or more words spelled and pronounced alike but different in meanings and origin. There are several pairs or groups of such words, only a few examples are given here. Note that they are different from **homophones.**

fleet (group of ships, planes, etc.)—*fleet* (move swiftly)—*fleet* (fast and nimble)
foot (low extremity of the leg on which an animal stands and walks)—*foot* (a unit of linear measure equaling 12 inches)
pole (long slender piece of wood or metal)—*pole* (extreme ends of Earth's axis)
quail (a game bird)—*quail* (feel or show fear)
rule (regulation within any sphere)—*rule* (thin printed line)—rule (exercise ultimate power over a people or nation)
sole (underside of a person's foot)—*sole* (one and only)
sow (plant seed)—*sow* (female pig)
train (teach a particular skill)—*train* (several railway carriages drawn by a locomotive)

Homophones are two or more words that are pronounced alike and have the same or similar sound but have different spellings and meaning. There are hundreds of such words and one should check the correct spelling for the required meaning if in doubt. Note the difference with *homonyms*.

berth (sleeping place in train, etc.)—B*irth* (coming into existence)
principal (head of an institution)—*Principle* (fundamental truth or belief)
sea (large expanse of saltwater)—*See* (power of discerning objects with eyes)
stationary (not moving)—*Stationery* (writing material)
weak (feeble)—*Week* (a period of seven days)

House and **home** are two nouns lightly used to mean the same thing, 'a dwelling place', but there is a subtle difference in usage. *House* could be any building, not necessarily as a living place for people (or animals) or a place of assembly; it sounds rather as an impersonal entity. *Home* is much more than a piece of architecture—it is a social entity constituted by a family or group living together, or a place of origin of a person or animals; it conjures up a vision of closeness and warmth and of a congenial environment or sanctuary—and has what you might call a 'soul'.

The *house* he built also has a garage for his car.
The *House* of Commons is the elected chamber of the British Parliament.
The green-*house* in the botanical garden houses exotic plants.
At Christmas we all assemble at the *home* of our parents.
Theirs is a happy *home*, full of love and consideration.
Her original *home* is in Delhi.
The salmon always return *home* to spawn.
The chicken always comes *home* to roost.
A new old age *home* has come up in the city.

However. The word means 'nevertheless' and 'in or to whatever manner or degree'. It can be used at the start of a sentence, in its middle or the end as appropriate.

However hard you may try you cannot break his resolve.
However, the meeting cold not be held because of lack of a quorum.
The meeting could not, *however*, be held because of lack of a quorum.
The meeting could not be held because of lack of a quorum, *however*.

Human; humane. *Human* is our own race of primates *Homo sapiens*, while *humane* is an adjective in respect of quality of compassion and sympathy for all living things.

Humans are the only bipeds, that is, animals that walk erect on two feet.
Animal right activists propagate *humane* treatment to all animals.

Hyperbaton is a figure of speech in which the normal order of words is inverted, especially for emphasis

The newborn is said to have six toes each—*this I must see.*
Musician you call yourself? Can you sing a note correctly?
I don't want to see her face—*she I hate.*

Hyperbole is a figure of speech in which there is a deliberate use of exaggeration for the sake of effect that is not meant to be taken literally. This is quite common both in speech and writing.

    He has *tons of money*. [A lot of money]
    She shed *bucketful of tears*. [Cried inconsolably]
    The new model Mercedes *costs a bomb*. [a great deal of money]
    The food in the restaurant *is to die for*. [extremely good or desirable; fabulous]

Hyphen is a punctuation mark used for compounding and joining two words together, and also sometimes of joining separated syllables of words broken at the end of a line to the beginning of the next. Two grammatically linked words are linked by a hyphen, but the current tendency is to write many without the hyphen. Some words with the prefix 're-' (meaning 'again') without the hyphen have different meaning and so the hyphen becomes necessary. A few examples are given here.

    recollect (remember)—*re-collect* (gather again)
    recover (to get back)—*re-cover* (cover again)
    reform (make change to improve)—*re-form* (form again)
    reprint (an offprint)—*re-print* (print again)
    reserve (to keep back)—*re-serve* (serve again)

Hyphenation of Numbers. A measure or object linking a number is hyphenated and is in the singular:

    The flag was hoisted on a *15-foot* pole. [not 'feet']
    The marathon was run on a *30-mile* course. [not 'miles']
    A *five-metre* tall statute of Mahatma Gandhi was erected at the crossing. [not 'metres']
    The police contingent is *25-man* strong. [not 'men']
    The milk is delivered in *5-litre* cans. [not 'litres']

I

I; me; myself. These pronouns create confusion in speaking and writing. *I* is now chiefly used as the subject of an immediately following verb, *me* occurs in every other position, and *myself* is used when the subject is referring to his/her oneself.

>Sushil and *I* are good friends.
>*I* invited him to come with *me* to the theatre.
>*I* carried out his orders.
>My wife and *I* went to the pictures last night.
>It is either he or *me*.
>You have got to include *me* in the project.
>His attack was directed at *me*.
>He is taller than *me*.
>I cut *myself* when peeling potatoes.
>I *myself* will take the car for repairs.
>I will take care of *myself* at the party.
>I am going to get *myself* a new car.

-ic and **–ical** are suffixes used with some nouns to form adjectives. In some nouns ending with *–y* both the forms can be used, like in *biography* (biographic/biographical), *biology* (biologic/biographical), *geography* (geographic/geographical) *geology* (geologic/ geological), *geomorphology* (geomorphologic/geomorphological), *palaeontology* (palaeontologic/palaeontological). The '*–ic*' ending is generally preferred by Americans. There are other nouns which admit of only one adjectival form, such as, *archaeology* (archaeological), *botany* (botanical), etc. A good dictionary should be consulted before the adjective is formed.

Idem. See **Instant...**

Idiom, Idioms. Simply put, idiom is specific character of a language or form of expression used by people for artistic expression; it may be peculiar to a people or nation. The English language has developed its own idiom in different nations. Good prose is idiomatic. There are numerous idiomatic phrases used in India; a few common ones are given here:

>*bag and baggage*
>*conspicuous by its absence*
>*fits and starts*
>*food for thought*

from top to bottom
hard and fast
high and dry
hither and thither
hue and cry
lock, stock and barrel
off the shelf
safe and sound
spick and span
take the bull by the horn
thick as thieves
to butter up
to keep the fingers crossed

Immoral; amoral. There is a slight distinction between these two words, and they are not interchangeable. *Immoral* means 'lack of morality due to wickedness or corruption'. *Amoral* denotes complete disregard of morality or any conduct outside morality.

In; Into. Both are function word which indicate inclusion, location or position within limits, but the two have different senses or nuances. *In* indicates that something or somebody is within or inside something. *Into* indicates that somebody or something is moving into something either physically or figuratively. Before using either word one should judge the circumstance in which it is being used.

He was hit *in* the leg
The letter was *in* English
The book is bound *in* cloth
He was *in* great hurry to catch the train.
The new car is *in* production
The new car will go *into* production next year
He went *into* the house
The vase broke *into* pieces
The party continued far *into* the night

In; into; on; at. These prepositions can be used both (i) in place and (ii) in time.

(1) Examples of in place usage:
She is in her office
He was wounded *in* his leg
He fell *into* the well
He is into the business of computers.
She is sitting *on* a chair
The plaster fell *on* her head.
He is sitting *at* his desk.
I met her *at* her home.

(2) Examples of in time usage:
>I bought the car *in* 1997.
>He was *in* time for the meeting.
>She did her paper *in* an hour.
>The work was expected to be completed by 1997 but it ran *into* early next year.
>The meeting started *on* time.
>They intend to open the shop *on* Sunday
>The bank opens *at* 10 a.m.

Indianism: Words and phrases of English which Indians have appropriated with altered meanings or concepts from that originally attributed or intended is Indianism. These are now acceptable as they are grammatically correct and are used widely. Some are given here.

air-dash = rush to some place by air.
>The minister *air-dashed* to the accident site.

bio-data = curriculum vitae; résumé
>Looking for a job he sent his *bio-data* to several companies.

blueprint = detailed plan or programme of action [expression derived from the blueprint used for copying maps and plans]
>A *blueprint* for the success of the scheme was drawn up by the director.

booth-capturing = forcibly seizing a voting booth to cast all votes in favour of a particular candidate.
>Heavy *booth-capturing* by the Samajwadi goons ensured his victory.

duplicate = fake; spurious; counterfeit (goods)
>Be careful, this market is full of *duplicate* goods.
>This watch is not original Rolex but a *duplicate*.

eve-teasing = publicly indecent teasing of girls and women.
>The Proctor caught four boys *eve-teasing* girls in the campus.

fall = long strip of cloth used for lining the lower border of a sari to make it 'fall' properly

half-pant = shorts, locally called nicker (knickers).
>The uniform of a RSS volunteer is khaki *half-pant* and white shirt.

high command = top decision-making people in a political party
>The Congress *high command* decided to field Rahul Gandhi from Rai Bareilly.

homely = home maker, good in household work [original meaning: plain or unattractive in appearance]
>I want a bride for my son who is *homely*, well-educated and beautiful.

land-shark = criminals who grab other's property
>The *land-sharks* in Mumbai grab a vacant land in connivance with local authorities.

Mafia/ mafa = any criminal or organized gang of criminals [adapted from Italian Mafia]
>The *mafia* in Mumbai are very powerful and run several smuggling rackets.
>The education *mafia* in U.P. organizes mass copying in Board examinations.

money laundering = device for converting illegal money into legally earned income that may be taxable.

Nursing Home = a small, private hospital [unlike in the West where it is an institution for the care of the elderly or terminally ill]
>After the accident she was rushed to the nearest *nursing home*.

out of station = away from his town of posting or residence
>She has gone *out of station* to attend to some work.

parallel economy = a black market economy that exists at the same time as a legal, open economy
>The *parallel economy* in India is believed to be of the same order as the legitimate one.

registry = registration of a document
>I got the *registry* done of the flat I bought recently.

roadside Romeo = a male person who teases a girl or woman publicly; a gay lothario.
>A *roadside Romeo* who was harassing girls in the bazaar was arrested by the police.

tom-tom = to declare openly [from tom-tom drum]
>He *tom-tommed* his success in examination by shouting from the roof top.

vote bank = a community, caste or group committed to vote en block
>The traders of the area are a committed *vote bank* of the Swatantra Party.

war footing = with urgent and accelerated effort as in war-time
>Breach in the dam was repaired on *war footing*.

wheatish complexion = off-white complexion.
>I am looking for a bride for my son who has *wheatish* complexion.]

with folded-hands = implies politeness, entreaty or surrender.
>I request you *with folded-hands* not to punish my son for not doing his homework.

Indianism: sentence construction that may not adhere to strict grammar or meaning but serves its purpose of expression. Such a sentence may be derived from the original thought in the mother tongue mentally translated into English and contains words that may be inappropriate synonyms or with somewhat altered shade of original meaning. One comes across such constructions in everyday conversations, but they are to be avoided in all serious writing. In the examples here the correct words or phrases are within square brackets.

Please write your phone number *behind* the cheque. [on the back or reverse of]
I *am not knowing* his address. [don't know]
I *am working* at the post office. [work]
I got shouted at by my boss. [my boss shouted at me]
He *passed out of* university. [graduated from]
She *had gone* to the doctor. [went]
There is no *time bounding*, take your time to finish the job. [binding of time...]

Indian words. The British colonials used numerous words from Indian languages and adopted some in toto and so integrated them that they are now bonafide words of standard English vocabulary, such as *bazaar, coolie, guru, jungle, pajamas, thug, verandah*, and numerous others. There are other words that have been incorporated in altered forms, like chintz (from *chhint*, a printed cloth), chit (from chitthi, a letter), cot (from *khat*), godown (from *godam*), muslin (from *malmal*), widow (from *vidhwa*) and many others. There are some other words with the original Indian meanings that have now come into style, such as *avatar, guru, karma, mantra, nirvana, pundit* and so on that are no longer italicised as foreign words. The process of incorporating Indian words is continuing. It is estimated that there are about 700 words in the *Oxford English Dictionary* that have been derived from Indian languages, but most are not understood beyond the Indian subcontinent. Other words are derivatives from the original Indian words such as follows:

Blighty = England or Britain [military slang from Hindi *Vilayati*]
calico = a type of cotton cloth [originally a cloth made in Calicut, Kerala]
indigo = dark blue dye [an agricultural product from India]
Juggernaut = huge and overwhelming force [from the enormous chariot of deity Jagannath in Puri, Orissa]
mufti = civilian clothes worn by a person in the armed forces [from the Indian word for 'free', indicating that the person was free not to wear the uniform]
shampoo = liquid preparation for washing hair [from Hindi *champu*, an act of head message by thumping]

Incompetent and **inefficient** are adjectives that denote different kinds of lack of capabilities and should be used carefully in describing a person's activity. *Incompetent* indicates a person who hasn't sufficient ability to do something successfully or effectively, while *inefficient* means that the person lacks capability of doing something in the required or desired manner.

> The carpenter I employed is a novice and is not *competent* to make good quality furniture.
> The carpenter I employed is very *inefficient* and took two days to make a simple stool.

Infectious and **contagious diseases.** These diseases are of different kinds. An *infectious disease* is liable to be transmitted or communicated through the environment, like plague, cholera, etc. A *contagious disease* is spread by direct or indirect contact of people or organisms, like common cold, influenza chicken and small pox, measles, etc.

Irony is expression whose apparent meaning is understood by a contrary meaning. It is an incongruity between an actual situation and expressed sentiment. It is used effectively to make a point forcefully, particularly in speech.

> It was snowing hard and he was holed up in his tent. In disgust he exclaimed: "Lovely weather, isn't it!'.
> Watching bikini-clad women on the beach, he remarked: "What a fashion parade!"
> His said too little by talking too much.
> Two students of theology were caught cheating in the examination.

Instant, idem, ultimo, proximo. Instead of clearly mentioning the month concerned many writers use these adverbs in their communications. *Instant* means 'the current month'; *idem*, 'the same month'; *ultimo*, the 'last month'; and *proximo*, 'of the next month'. In a communication, these words could cause confusion because the recipient has to consult the date of communication before he can gauge the month to which the matter refers. This style becomes particularly irksome in a long write-up. The abbreviations *inst.*, *ult.*, and *prox.* are often used instead of the full form. It is better to write the month in full.

Invite is a verb, but is now frequently used informally as a noun for written 'invitation'. Though it is inelegant, it has come widely into general use.

-ise versus **-ize.** There is some problem as to which of these two spellings should be used in words ending with 'z' sound: 'ize' or '-ise' (for example: *organize* or *organise*). Most dictionaries give the spelling of many such words with the letter 'z'. The standard Americans spelling of such words is with 'z', and Microsoft Word (default) dictionary shows such words as incorrect if typed with 's'. But in several countries like Britain, Australia and India such words are spelt with 's', supported by several authorities though the Concise Oxford Dictionary too spells such words with 'z'. Some confusion arises when words like *advertise, comprise, despise, exercise* and *surmise* are used universally with 's', including the United States. So, to avoid confusion it is safer that all words with such endings should uniformly be spelled with '-ise- to solve the problem of remembering which ending to use with which word.

Isn't it? This general phrase is quite common in India to ask after a yes/no question. Each question requires a separate grammatical response depending on the subject of the enquiry. The correct enquiry to make after each statement

is italicised in the following examples and not the general phrase 'isn't it?'
You are gong to marry Shika, *aren't you?*
This bus goes to Kanpur, *doesn't it?*
Some schools charge a heavy fee, *don't they?*
The budget gave further relief to women and senior citizens, *did it?*
We had fun playing football, *didn't we?*
This is a remake of an old film, *isn't it?* [Here 'isn't it' is appropriate]

Italian words. A selection of words from the Italian often used in English are given here. They are not italicized as foreign.

Ditto/ditto = substitute for repetition of a word or phrase
fiasco = complete failure or breakdown
graffiti = a writing or drawing on some public surface like a wall or rock.
imbroglio = a violently complicated altercation
incognito = with one's true identity concealed
inferno = hell; intense heat
lingua franca = a common language between speakers whose native languages are different [originally a common language consisting of Italian with another language]
Mafia = concealed criminal organization [from the secret criminal society of Sicily or Italy]
manifesto = a written document declaring publicly the policy or aim of its issuer
medico = physician; medical student
motto = a short phrase or sentence indicating a belief or ideal
numero uno = number one; the very top
prima donna = main female singer in opera; temperamental person
propaganda = information, especially biased and misleading, spread deliberately to further apolitical cause or a point of view
torso = sculptured trunk of a human body
vista = distant view through an avenue or opening.

Italics. Words and phrases from foreign languages are generally printed in such slanting types—and underlined in manuscript—, but now-a-days the practice is that such words and phrases that have become common in English writing are increasingly being printed in the normal Roman type. Words and phrases requiring emphasis may be italicized in a sentence or a dialogue for effect. (In examples given in this work italics have been used to point out the relevant word or phrases.) In a text, titles of books, journals, movies, poems, paintings, ships, etc., are generally italicized. Letters that form an acronym are italicised, too. In biological writing the Latin names of genera and species are always italicized- but in hand-written or typed communications the intended italic words or letters are underlined.

> I have made it clear to him that he will *not* be allowed to go on leave now.
> William Shakespeare's play *Merchant of Venice* was staged in the school.
> Stephen Hawkings's *A Brief History of Time* is a science classic.
> *Gitanjali* got Rabindra Nath Tagore the Nobel Prize for Literature.
> *Sedimentary Rocks* by F. J. Pettijohn is the best text book on the subject.
> I subscribe to the *Journal of the Geological Society of India*.
> The article was published in *The Times of India*.
> *India Today* is a popular weekly magazine.
> *Sholay* is considered the most notable Indian movie.
> The only aircraft carrier with the Indian Navy is *INS Vikrant*.
> Radar is an acronym formed from *r*adio *d*etecting *a*nd *r*anging.
> The scientific name of the mango plant is *Mangifera indica*.

But the names of religious books are *not* italicized.

The Bible	The New Testament
The Qur'an	The Avesta
The Bhagwad Gita	The Vedas
The Ramayana	The Mahabharata

In biological nomenclature, the names of genera and species are printed in italics, the generic name is capitalized and the specific name is in lower case even if the name is taken after a person or locality:

The scientific name of humans is *Homo sapiens*.

The delectable mango goes by the scientific name of *Mangifera indica*.

A well-known Indian fossil of elephant is called *Stegedon ganesa*.

[Note that though the specific part of the Linnean nomenclature is taken after a personal name, Ganesha, the word is not capitalized. The same is true of *indica* which is after India.]

Its, It's. The usage of these two constructions causes a lot of confusion and they are quite often used incorrectly. *Its* is a possessive determiner meaning 'relating to, belonging to or associated with an object or action previously mentioned'. With the apostrophe, *it's* is a contraction of 'it is' or it has'. A little thought will show the proper use of the two variants.

I put the dog in *its* kennel'.

The child is very proud of *its* bicycle.

This is Bengali food at *its* best.

It's a book-lovers paradise.

Now *it's* your turn to strike the ball'.

It's possible that he may join the party.

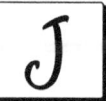

Japanese words. Some words from Japanese language have recently been adopted in English vocabulary, while other words describe popular things like bonsai, haiku, ikebana, karate, kimono, sushi, tofu and tsunami.

hara-kiri = A ritual suicide by the Japanese, but now used in English as a general term for 'suicide'
   Failing in the examination, the emotionally disturbed boy committed *hara-kiri*.

honcho = a boss or big-shot
   The head *honcho* of this enterprise is a slave-driver.

sayonara = Final Goodbye
   After the break she said *sayonara* to her boy friend.

tycoon = A businessman or industrialist of exceptional wealth and power
   He is a big business *tycoon*.

Jargon is confused, unintelligible language. The term is also used for scientific, technical, medical or professional terminology of a special group or activity which is hardly understood by those outside its charmed circle. Here is a good examples from the world of cricket:
   He made a *ton* [hundred] in the first inning, but was out for a *duck* [zero] in the second.

Joy and **pleasure** are words indicating emotions of happiness or delight but have fine shades of meaning. *Joy* is indicative of happiness which comes from the heart, while *pleasure* is sensual gratification that is something felt physically. These words should be used with some discrimination. *Delight* is a word which covers both the emotions of joy and pleasure to a high degree.
   The birth of a son filled her with unbound *joy*.
   It is a *joy* to behold a rainbow in the sky.
   It is a great *pleasure* to dine at this fine restaurant.
   It is my *pleasure* to accept your invitation.
   It is always a *joy* and *pleasure* to meet old friends after a long absence.
   She was *delighted* when she was invited to perform at the Rashtrpati Bhawan.

Judicial; judicious. These two adjectives are often confused. While *judicial* refers mainly to legal processes, *judicious* means 'having or showing sound judgment'.
   The *judicial* process in getting a house vacated by a tenant is very cumbersome.
   The *judicious* use of the funds by the committee resulted in getting two wells constructed instead of one as planned.

Knights and Baronets (British). Although no Indian is allowed to accept a foreign title after Independence, we still encounter those who were knighted by the British monarch Knights and Baronets are entitled to use the title *Sir* before their names. Indians often make mistakes in referring to or addressing knights and baronets. It may be noted that the title *Sir* is used before the given name and not before the surname. The full style of writing a knight's name is, for example:

Sir Vidiadhur Surajprasad Naipaul or Sir V. S. Naipaul
But he will be addressed as:
Sir Vidiadhur/Vidia [and NOT as Sir Naipaul]
If there is any other tile before the name of a *knight*, it will precede *Sir*, as follows:
Dr Sir Vidia Naipaul
His wife will be referred to as
    Lady Naipaul or Lady Nadira Naipaul
But never as
    Lady Nadira

[It may be noted that Lady title before a woman's given name can only be used for the unmarried daughters of a duke, marquis or earl of British nobility.]

Late; lately. The adjective *late* means 'after the right time', but the adverb lately has the meaning of 'in recent times'.
>I was *late* for the office
>It has been noticed *lately* that some clerks are always *late* for the office.

Latin Words and phrases. Numerous words and phrases in the English language are derived or used in original from Latin; several are used in the legal profession. Though foreign words, they are generally not italicized.

a priori = from cause to effect
ad hoc = for this particular purpose
ad interim = for the interim time
ad lib/ad libitum = improvised, without preparation
ad nauseum = to a disgusting extent
ad valorem = in proportion to estimated value of goods
alma mater = educational istitution which one has attended
as infinitum = without limit
certiorari = writ from higher court for record of casetried in lower court
cum laude = with distinction
curriculum vitae = brief acount of one's career
de faco = in fact, whether by right or not
de novo = new; startingfresh
ex gracia = as an ac of favour or grace; without acceptance of liability
ex officio = by virtue of an office
ex post facto = retrospectively
habeas corpus = writ requiring person to be produced before judge or court
honoris causa = as a mark of esteem
in situ = in the original place
inter alia = among other things
ipso facto = by that very fact
locus standi = recognized or right position
mandamus = superior court's writ conveying command to lower court
modus operendi = method of operation of a person, like a criminal, about a task;
mutatis mutandis = with due alteration of detail

nisi = (decree/rule) subject to conditions as regards taking effect
pari passu = simultaneously
per diem = for each day
per se = by or in itself
persona non grata = person not acceptable, especially diplomat
pro forma = a standard document or form
pro rata = proportional
quod vide = which see (reference)
sensu stricto = in strict or narrow sense
sic = written exactly as in the original [often written within square brackets]
sine die = adjourned indefinitely
sine qua non = essential condition or qualification
status quo = existing state of affairs
subpoena (pronounced *sepina*). A writ ordering a person to attend the court.
suo motu = in its own accord
terra ferma = firm ground, the Earth
Vide = see specified passage in book or work
viva voce = oral examination
volte-face = complete change of argument, politics, etc.
vox populi = people's voice; public opinion
There are certain Latin phrases which are used generally in abbreviation only:
Quod erat demonstratum (QED) = which was to be proved is done
Requiescat in peace (RIP) = may he/she rest in peace

Lawful; legal; legitimate. There is a fine distinction between the three words, all indicating 'in accordance with law'. *Lawful* means 'in conformity with law or rule of any kind'; *legal* implies 'in conformity of law as administered by courts', and *legitimate* has the wider meaning even of 'any right supported by tradition or custom'.

> The protest march by the union during the lunch break was perfectly *lawful*.
> Marriage of people from different communities is perfectly *legal* in India.
> The claim of compensation as demanded by him is *legitimate* as he was not given any opportunity to defend himself.

Lay is a verb which has the essential meaning of 'to put down'. Its past and past participle is **laid.** Verbal phrases formed from *lay* have different meanings.

> The minister *laid* the foundation of a new school building.
> The municipality has decided to *lay* a new road in the colony.
> The principal *laid* emphasis on good behaviour by the students.
> She has *laid* claim to a share in the ancestral property.
> A table for two was *laid* for the young couple.

lay aside means essentially 'to put away'.
: He has *laid aside* a substantial amount of money for his retirement.

lay down means 'to establish' or 'to surrender':
: The Principal has *laid down* a rule that every student must clean his/her desk after class.
: The dacoits *laid down* their arms when surrounded by the police.

lay in means 'to accumulate':
: They *laid in* all essential supplies for the fear of an indefinite strike by the truckers.

lay off means 'to remove' or 'to quit':
: The *lay off* became inevitable when the company started running into loss.
: He *laid off* smoking after he was diagnosed with lung disease.

lay on means 'to give' or 'to provide':
: A layer of asphalt was *laid on* the surface to make the road motorable.
: A sumptuous breakfast was *laid on* for the guests.

lay out means 'to display':
: A map of the newly proposed township was *laid out* for inspection.

lay up means 'to amass':
: She is getting old and has *laid up* a good deal of money for her retirement.

Lead; led. Both are pronounced 'led'. The verb *lead* roughly means 'to conduct' or 'guide', and its past participle is *led*.

Lessee, lessor. The two words have entirely different meanings but are often confused. *Lessee* is one that holds real or personal property under a lease. Lessor is one that gives property on lease.

Let. This is a verb which has several meanings like 'to allow, enable, cause, grant' and so on. *Let* has the same past and past participle forms. Verbal phrases formed from *let* have different shades of meaning.
: She could not *let* show go this opportunity to make a few extra bucks.
: Please *let* me know when I should contact you.
: *Let* me try for this job though I know that the competition is tough.
: I believe in the motto '*to* live and to *let* live'.

let down means 'to betray, fail or disappoint'
: She was badly *let down* when she was denied promotion though earlier the boss had promised.

let in means 'to admit' or 'to include ':
: There was pandemonium in the stadium when the management *let in* more people than it could hold.

let off means 'to release' or 'to discharge'
: The prisoner was *let off* for want of evidence.

let out means 'to give', and is often used for 'giving on rent':
>She *let out* a scream of joy when she won the beauty pageant.
>The premises were *let out* on a consideration of Rs. 5000 per month.

let up means 'to decrease' or 'to halt':
>There was no *let up* in protests even after their demand was conceded.

Lexicon in essence is a dictionary, particularly of a special discipline or field of knowledge. It is also the **vocabulary** of a language.

Liable; likely. These two words are used sometimes interchangeably with the preposition 'to' but the meanings are different. Liable means 'legally or otherwise bound', while *likely* means 'probably'.
>You are *liable* to be fined for wrong parking.
>He is *liable* to damages if he breaks the contract.
>He is *likely* to address the gathering this evening.
>He is *likely* to be available tomorrow for discussion.

License; Licence. These two words pronounced the same and differing very slightly in spelling has been a source of confusion for long. In British English, *licence* is the noun and *license* is the verb. On the other hand, in American English, *license* is both the noun and the verb. Now, the American spelling prevails, though in India we have a 'driving licence'.
>On reaching the age of 18, he got himself a *driving licence*. [license]
>The new hotel is now *licensed* to sell liquor.

Ligature. See **Diphthong**.

Lighting; lightning. These two words appear similar but have different meanings. *Lighting* is 'the effect of lights as illumination', and *lightning* is the natural phenomenon of 'the high voltage electrical flashes between a cloud and the ground'.

Litotes is a figure of speech where a deliberate understatement is made for the sake of effect.
>Climbing this peak is not an easy task. (Climbing this peak is quite difficult.)
>He is not a bad singer. (Patronizing statement that he is a passable accomplished singer.)

Little; a little; the little. *Little* means 'small' and suggests that there is not very much or hardly any in terms of quantity, if there is any. With the introduction of the indefinite article, *a little* has the positive meaning of 'a small quantity' and suggests that while there is not much, there is at least some. With the definite article, the little denotes 'the small quantity'. [see also **Few**]
>It is a matter of concern that she has made *little* progress in the class. [practically no progress]
>There is *little* hope for her recovery after the accident. [practically no hope]

She has *little* money to buy a new dress. [hardly any]
It is good that she has made *a little* progress in her class. [some progress]
There is *a little* hope that she may recover after the accident. [some hope]
She has *a little* money to buy a new dress. [some money]
The little progress she could make was all due to the effort of the tutor she engaged. [whatever progress]
She spent *the little* money she had on a new dress. [small quantity]

Look is a verb that essentially means 'to see'; its past tense and past participle is the same **looked**. Verbal phrases formed from *look* have different meanings.

look after means 'to care for'. .
In her old age she was *looked after* by her son.

look down on means 'despise'.
He is a snob and *looks down* on his subordinates

look forward means 'to await'.
She is *looking forward* to a visit to Maldives during the summer vacations.

look into means 'to examine'.
The manager assured her that he would *look into* her grievances.

look out means 'to watch out'.
She is *looking out* for a maid good in housework

look over means 'to examine'.
He decided to *look over* several models before deciding to buy a new car.

look up means 'to seek out'.
When I go to Delhi I will *look up* my old college friend.

look up to means 'to respect'.
They *look up to* their teacher for guidance.

Lunch; Luncheon. *Lunch* is a meal taken in the middle of the day, and *luncheon* is the same meal but a formal one as a part of a meeting or other special occasion.

Majority; minority can be both as singular or plural words, and then take the appropriate verb. Singular verb is used if the things and people are considered as a group, but plural verb is used if they re considered individually.

> The *majority* in the company *want* a five-day week. [majority = maximum number as a group]
> A *majority* of people *have* voted for him. [majority = large number of individuals]
> The *minority* status of the school *has* been recognized by the government. [minority = a group]
> A *minority* of shareholders *were* always opposed to the proposal but could do nothing. [minority = small individuals]

Make is verb that has several meanings like 'to build or create', 'to accomplish', 'to compel', 'to appoint', 'to service' and so on. Its past and past participle is **made**. Verbal phrases formed from *make* have different meanings.

> The scientists have *made* a robot that can walk and climb stairs.
> His new motorbike *makes* such a racket that the neighbours are complaining.
> He *made* to the top in his company by sheer hard work.
> The shop was *made* to replace the defective machine by the Consumer Forum.
> She was *made* the manager despite objections by some members of the board.
> After being snow-bound for days the mountaineers could *make* it to the base camp with difficulty.

make for means 'to move towards'.
> As soon as the dinner was announced, everybody *made for* the buffet tables.

make off means 'to leave in haste'.
> The man snatched the purse of the lady and *made off* before he could be apprehended.

make off with means 'to grab'.
> The thief *made off with* all the valuables he could find in the house.

make out means 'to detect'.
> I really don't know if you can *make out* anything from this document.

make up means 'to create' or 'to decide'.
> The special train was *made up* of ten air-conditioned bogies.
> She had already *made up* her mind to emigrate to Australia.

make up for means 'to compensate for'.
> The company *made up for* the oversight by paying cash for the missing items.

make up to means 'to flatter'.
> After the quarrel he tried to *make up to* her by sending her a dozen roses.

Malapropism. Amusing misuse of vocabulary when a similarly sounding but inaccurate word is used. This word was coined after Mrs. Melaprop, a character in Sheridan's play 'The Rivals', who kept on this verbal confusion in her speech.
> I have come to *condone* the death of your mother. [condole]
> He is a big business *typhoon*. [tycoon]
> She is the wife of a big textile *magnet* from Bombay. [magnate]
> In our garden we have flowers of all colours of the *rectum*. [spectrum]

Manuscript is a handwritten document, composition or text, particularly for publication, abbreviated to 'MS'. With the introduction of the typewriter, hand-written documents for publication became a rarity, and with a printer linked to the computer hand-written matter for the printer is now practically extinct. The typewritten material submitted for printing is now referred to sometimes as 'TS', but the abbreviation 'MS' is still preferred by the printer for typewritten material as well—anyway, there is hardly any handwritten matter now submitted. The plural of the abbreviation is 'MSS'.

Many denotes great but indefinite in numbers, as in "many times". But when there is one of a large but indefinite number it could also be put thus: *many a time'*— which is singular and takes a singular verb as the verb is for the noun and not for the adjective 'many'. When in doubt remember that there is the singular 'a' after many.
> *Many* towns were ravaged by the floods.
> Many a town was ravaged by the floods. [Not: Many a town were ...]
> There's *many a* slip 'twixt the cup and the lip'.

May, might. Both the words express 'possibility'. *May* suggests 'more or less great possibility', and *might* a 'distant possibility'
> He *may* not have time to meet you.
> You *may* go home now.
> He *might* meet you if he has time.
> You *might* as well go home.

Maxim. See **Proverb...**

Meantime; meanwhile. Both the words mean 'during the intervening time', but they are used in different ways. *Meantime* is a noun, and is used with the phrase 'in the meantime' or 'for the meantime'. Meanwhile is an adverb and is used alone.
> *In the meantime*, she decided to join a dance class.
> *Meanwhile*, she decided to join a dance class.

Media is now associated with agencies of mass communication. Though *media* is the plural of 'medium', it is in practice used as a singular noun with the plural formed as 'medias', and there is also 'mediums'.

> Television is now a *media* of mass communication.
> Both the electronic and print *medias* gave prominence to the news.
> The print *medium* is more suitable for propagating his views.
> For propagating his views he uses both the *mediums*, TV and newspapers.

Meiosis is a figure of speech in which an understatement is made.

> The brave soldier was badly bleeding in his leg but with a feeble laugh he said not to worry as it was only *a little scratch*.
> The billionaire Ambanis lost a million but for them it's just *a little loose change*.
> To a hardened gambler losing a thousand rupees is but *chickenfeed*.
> For an avid mountaineer like him a frostbite is but *a little inconvenience*.

Metaphor is 'implied simile'. For example :

> Her stone heart showed no reaction. (Metaphor)
>
> (Her heart is compared to a stone.)
> He is as brave as a lion. (Simile)
> He is a lion. (Metaphor)

Metathesis is accidental transportation of words which can be considered as a kind of **spoonerism**.

> I am going to plant my water today. [I am going to water my plant today.]
> I need to put these eyes thrice in the drops daily. [I need to put these drops thrice in the eyes daily.]

Metonymy is a figure of speech where a person or thing is not named directly but by some associated thing or attribute. (*See also* **Euphuism**)

> The prisoner appeared before the *bench*. [judge].
> The *men in khaki* [policemen] then baton-charged the crowd.
> He took to the *bottle* [liquor] after the death of his wife.
> He was an avid reader of *Shakespeare*. [the works of Shakespeare]
> A communiqué from the *Rashtrpati Bhawan* announced the appointment of five Ministers of State with independent charge. [the President of India]

Million and **Billion**. The value of a million universally means 1,000,000 (10^6). The value of a *billion* in USA and France is a thousand million (10^9) and of a *trillion*, a million million (10^{12}), but a *billion* in UK and Germany is a million million (12^{12}), and a *trillion* is a million million million (10^{18}). However, universally the American definitions have come to be accepted and used.

Miss; Mrs., Ms. Though *Mr.* is the title used for all males, two different titles are used for women depending on their marital status. *Miss* is used before the name of an unmarried woman or girl, and *Mrs.* for married women. *Ms.* (pronounced *Miz*) has now been introduced to get rid of this distinction. There is often a problem in the proper use of a title before the name of a married woman who uses her maiden name for professional or other purposes. In such a case it is proper to use the title *Miss*.

> *Miss* Benazir Bhutto. [Not: *Mrs.* Benazir Bhutto. But: *Mrs.* Benazir Zardari or *Mrs.* Asif Zardari]

Mixed Metaphor is a combination of incongruous or ludicrous metaphors that are unrelated, and should be avoided.

> He hit the ball for a six and took the bull by the horn.
> He bit the hand that rocks the cradle.
> If you shirking work, your bread and butter will be cut right out under your feet.
> You can lead a gift horse to water but you can't look in its mouth.

Moral; morale. These two words have related concerns. *Moral* as adjective is 'concerned with right and wrong conduct or behaviour' and as noun refers to 'the lesson derived from a fable, incident, experience, etc.' *Morale* is a noun meaning 'discipline and spirit that pervades a person or group'.

> The students are taught the basic *moral* vales of truthfulness and honesty.
> The *moral* of the story is that it does not pay to tell lies.
> Although she is confined to a wheel chair her *morale* is very high and she cheerfully does all the tasks assigned to her.
> After wining at the Asian Games the *morale* of the team was high and the players were raring to take on any team at the Olympics.
> Though the conditions at the Siachin Glacier are truly harsh the *morale* of our jawans there is very high.

Myself, and similar Pronouns. Sometimes these long pronounces are used where a simple one would do better.

Myself   = I (or me)
Yourself   = you
Herself   = she (or her)
Himself   = he (or him)
Itself   = it
Ourselves = we (or us)
Yourselves = you
Themselves = they (or them)

However, the self forms are correct additions for emphasis:

> I hurt *myself*.
> You *yourself* spoke to him.
> She *herself* did not know.
> He could not help *himself*.
> It cannot stand by *itself*.
> We *ourselves* witnessed the scene.
> You *yourself* agreed to buy.
> They *themselves* are to blamed.

Names, Proper, as attributes. There are some people, real or fictional, who have given their names as words that signify their special character or attribute. The words are capitalized.

Boswell. James Boswell (18th century) is famous for recording in the biography of his mentor Dr. Samuel Johnson the most trivial of details. Whenever a person pens an intimate biography of his admirer he is referred to as 'he is a Boswell to his Johnson'.
> Patrick French is Sir V. S. Naipaul's *Boswell* as he has written an intimate biography of the writer.

Casanova. The legendary 19th century Italian adventurer Giacomo Casanova was a promiscuous and unscrupulous seducer of women and has given his name to a man with this character.
> He is a *Casanova* who tries to seduce every woman he meets at a party.

Don Juan. A legendary 19th century Spaniard considered a great lover and seducer of women, has now become synonymous for a person possessing such qualities.
> He is quite a *Don Juan* on the campus and keeps seducing the sophomores.

Frankenstein. A fictional monster created by Mary Shelly in a novel that has become a synonym for 'a monstrous creature that ruins the originator'.
> The United States created the Taliban which became a *Frankenstein* that later destroyed its erstwhile patron.

Houdini. Harry Houdini was an internationally known magician reputed as a great escape artist. So, when some one disappears from a difficult situation he is said to have 'done a Houdini'.
> When the police went to arrest him the terrorist from his hideout did a *Houdini*.

Jughead is a character in Archie Comics who is for ever hungry and craves for food all the time. So a compulsive foodie is called so.
> The little boy is a thorough *Jughead* who is hungry all the time.

Lilliputian. The name of the fictional island in Jonathan swift's novel *Gulliver's Travels* whose inhabitants were six-inches tall. The word Lilliputian has now come to mean 'very small'.
> In Hindi literature he stands so tall that other writers look like *Lilliputians* before him.

Mrs Grundy is a fictional character in Thomas Morton's 1798 play *Speed the Plough* and her attribute as a person employing conventional propriety and prudery is used to describe a woman having the same characteristics.
> Our neighbour Mrs. Sharma is a regular *Mrs. Grundy* and keeps interfering with the youngsters in our locality.

Shylock is a character in Shakespeare's *The Merchant of Venice* who is an extortionist moneylender and is now considered an epitome of greed.
> The village moneylender is an unscrupulous *Shylock* who deprives his clients even of the last vestige of clothes from their body.

Samson is a biblical hero with great strength. [also adjective samsonian meaning a person of great strength]
> This wrestler is a *Samson* who can demolish his opponents with the swipe of his left hand. [The wrestler has Samsonian strength.]

Names, Proper, now regular words. There are several words which originally were proper nouns (names of people or places) but have become regular words for that object and are not capitalized.

Balaclava = a type of headgear (after a place in Crimea peninsula in SE Europe]
Chesterfield = a kind of overcoat and also furniture (after Lord Chesterfield)
China = porcelain ware made from a special type of clay originally from China
Cologne = perfume toilet water (after the city of Cologne, Germany
Macadam = Broken stone with bitumanised binder for paving roads (after British engineer John L. McAcadam)
Mackintosh = cloth waterproofed by rubber (after British chemist Charles Mackintosh)
Martinet = a strict disciplinarian [after the French general Jean Martinet, a strict disciplinarian]
Maverick = an unorthodox person [from the Texas rancher Samuel A. Maverick
who did not brand his cattle]
Sandwich = food item of two slices of bread with relish in-between (after its originator Earl of Sandwich)

Neither as a pronoun meaning 'not one or the other of the two or more' it is generally used with a singular verb, but the plural verb can also be used depending on usage.
> Neither side of the dispute *was* willing for a compromise.
> Neither of the disputants *were* willing to a compromise.

None is not a contraction of 'no one', and is used in two senses: (1) none = not one; (2) none = no persons or things. In the first sense it takes a singular verb:

None of the teachers *was* present in the school.

In the second sense it takes a plural verb:
None have been allowed to take the examination.
None of the devises have safety features.

North is not only a direction of the compass but has also acquired other meanings in the current parlance. *North* is also used to describe 'the industrially and economically developed nations of the world'. In the modern language of economics it means 'higher' or 'increasing', and adverb 'northward' is formed from it. {See entry below]

Unfortunately, the patronising attitude of the *North* towards developing economies is not helping matters.
The recent abnormal *northward* rise of oil prices has sent economies of some African countries in a tailspin.
Due to inflation the prices of all commodities are going *north*.

Northward; northwards; northerly; northern. The writer gets perplexed by the correct use of the first two words. *Northward* is adjective and adverb both, meaning 'in a northerly direction' and *northwards* is adverb only meaning 'towards the north'. Since the sense is the same either could be used. *Northerly* has the meaning of 'in a northward position or direction' or 'coming from the north' with particular reference to the wind. Northern means 'situated in or facing the north.

The northward trek brought them to the ruins.
If you look *northwards* you can see the ruins in the distance.
The *northerly* wind brought snow and sleet.
The *northern* part of Canada lies within the Arctic Circle.

Noted; notable; noteworthy; noticeable. As adjectives these similar-looking words essentially have the sense of 'well-known' or 'evident'. *Noted* means 'eminent' or celebrated'. *Notable* and *noteworthy* are synonyms meaning 'worthy of notice' and are applicable to both people and events. The same is true of *noticeable* which means 'obvious' or 'perceptible'.

She is a *noted* gynecologist known for pioneering work in pre-natal care.
Her *notable* work lies in the field of child care.
The building of a helipad on the Siachin glacier is a *notable* achievement.
Her work in the field of child care is *noteworthy*.
The building of a helipad on the Siachin glacier is a *noteworthy* achievement.
The improvement in her condition is quite *noticeable*.
There were *noticeable* errors in the proofs sent by the press.

Nouns, collective. One is often confused whether to use the singular verb 'has' and 'is', or to the plurals 'have' and 'are' with collective words like parliament, government, department, committee, police and the like. Either seems proper but the plural verbs seem to be more in use in many cases. Moreover, when a pronoun has to be used it appears more natural to use the plural form.

> The government *has* approved the mid-day meal scheme.
> The government *is* in two minds about waving off the loans.
> The police *are* perfectly capable of controlling the crowds.
> *They are* perfectly capable of controlling the crowds.
> The police *has* cordoned off the area where the bomb blast took place.
> Te committee *has* decided to dispense with his services.
> *They have* taken a decision to dispense with his services.

Nouns always written in plural. Several objects that are one single entity with two identical parts are written in plural, often preceded by the phrase 'pair of…'.

> I saw a new species of the bird through my *binoculars*.
> I now have a new *pair of binoculars*.
> The *scissors* used by the village tailor have rusted.
> The tailor bought a new *pair of scissors*.
> The doctor says that I need to have new *spectacles*.
> I got a new *pair of spectacles*.
> He had to wade through slush and his *trousers* got dirty.
> The new *pair of trousers* that he bought don't fit properly.

Nouns only singular. There are some nouns for which there are no plural forms, and take a singular verb.

> The *debris* from the mine *was* removed by shovels.
> The procurement of *wheat is* taken over by the government.
> *Milk is* good for growing children

Nouns only plural. Some nouns are only in the plural though they are singular in construction.

> The *billiards* table has been damaged.
> The *news* about the disaster was flashed on the TV.
> *Economics* is one of the subjects taught in the college.
> The *mathematics* paper was very difficult.
> The *measles* epidemic has taken several lives.

Nouns both singular and plural. There are other nouns which are used both as singular and plural depending on the context.

> The first *series* of the journal *was* issued in 1975.
> Two *series* of the journal *are* brought our each year.
> A single *species* of the plant *is* known to occur in the Himalayas.
> Several *species* of the plant *are* known to occur in the Himalayas.

Numerical Expressions. In a sentence numbers one through nine are spelled out in words, as also those numbers of one hundred or over that can be written in two words, but not in mathematical or statistical reports. Full and higher numbers are written in numerals.

Only *six* questions are to be answered.
The train was late by about *three-and-a-half* hours.
The van can accommodate only *10* people.
Some *three hundred* scientists are expected to attend the conference.
There were 317 *passengers in the liner when it sank.*

But figures are used to express dimensions, distances and other quantities in a sentence:
A distance of *10* miles and *3* furlongs has to be covered.
It is *2* feet and *10* inches long.
Kanpur is *84* km from Lucknow.
A *10*-km road was laid out.
The engine has *100* horsepower.
His sight is good at *10/10* vision.

If there are fractions or decimal points in a figure, numerals could be used.
3   7½   10
3.25   7.5   10.75
The conversion factor of one inch to a metric unit is *25.4* mm exactly.

The numbers at the beginning of a sentence should be spelled out in full and not in digits:
Two hundred scientists are expected to attend the symposium.
Forty-four is the total membership of the club.

Numerals, India. The whole system of nomenclature of higher Indian units of numbers is given below. However, in common practice the nomenclature up to *crore* only is used, though the unit *arab* may be mentioned sometimes. The rest of the unit names are not in use, the higher values may be expressed in *crores* only. The entire nomenclature of higherachy of Indian units is generally not known and is printed here for record only to ensure that it is not lost to posterity.

Unit	*Factor*	*Value*
Lakh	10^5	1,00,000
Crore	10^7	1,00,00,000
Arab	10^9	1,00,00,00,000
Kharab	10^{11}	1,00,00,00,00,000
Neel	10^{13}	1,00,00,00,00,00,000
Padam	10^{15}	1,00,00,00,00,00,00,000
Sankh	10^{17}	1,00,00,00,00,00,00,00,000

In actual practice values higher than crore are expressed in hundreds, thousands (and so on) crores:

1,00,00,00,000	=	100 crores (hundred crores)
10,00,00,00,000	=	1,000 crores (one thousand crores)
10,00,00,00,00,000	=	1,00,000 crores (one lakh crores)

Numerals, Roman. Roman numerals are confusing and it is best to avoid them but they are even now used to number volumes, chapters, plates of illustrations, tables, etc, in books and other publications. The greatest disadvantage of Roman numerals is that they cannot be used in mathematical exercises, even for simple additions and subtractions.

Letters, either capitals or lower case, are used in place of numbers in Roman numerals and act as symbols. The value of the basic Roman letter symbols are given below:

I	=	1
V	=	5
X	=	10
L	=	50
C	=	100
D	=	500
M	=	1000

In place of capital letters as above, lower case letters *i, v, x, l, c, d* and *m* can also be used, generally to number preliminary and Index pages in books, or in the middle of text within parentheses where serial numbers are required.

To make certain numbers intermediate between the two main symbols the value of a letter symbol preceding one of the greater value is subtracted, and the symbol is placed left of the greater symbol. Some examples are:

IV	=	4	(5 minus 1)
IX	=	9	(10 minus 1)
XL	=	40	(50 minus 10)
CD	=	400	(500 minus 100)
CM	=	900	(1000 minus 100)

The value of a letter symbol following another of the same or grater value is placed right of the greater number symbol, as:

III	=	3	(1+1+1)
VII	=	7	(5+1+1)
XVI	=	16	(10+5+1)
LXXII	=	72	(50+10+10+1+1)
CLXVI	=	166	(100+50+10+5+1)
DCLXII	=	662	(500+100+50+10+1+1)
MDCCCLXXXVI	=	1886	(1000+500+100+100+100+50+10+10+10+5+1)

It can be seen from the above that any number of several digits can be obtained by combination of the above two procedures. It may be noted that for subtraction only one letter symbol on the left can be used, but there is no lime for additional symbols on the right.

Letter symbol *I* can be placed before *V* or *X* only once; symbol *X* can be placed before *L* or *C* only once; symbol *C* can be placed before *D* or *M* only once

IV	=	4
IX	=	9
XL	=	40
XC	=	90
CD	=	400
CM	=	900

Symbols *I, X, C* and *M* may be repeated twice or thrice to double or triple the values, but <u>not</u> symbols *V, L* or *D:*

II	=	2
III	=	3
XX	=	20
XXX	=	30
CC	=	200
CCC	=	300
MM	=	2000
MMM	=	3000

ಶ್ರೀ

Obstinate; obdurate; stubborn . These adjective mean the same: 'unreasonably or perversely unyielding'. *Obstinate* implies an unreasonable persistence. *Obdurate* implies resistance to persuasion or inflexibility. *Stubborn* implies resistance to change and applies to people and objects.

>Despite an apology by him, she *obstinately* demanded his dismissal.
>He is so *obdurate* that he refuses to change his view in spite of evidence to the contrary.
>She is too *stubborn* to admit that she was wrong.
>She had such a *stubborn* cold that it did not go away despite best treatment.

Officialese is a language frequently used by public or government officials which is verbose, pompous and often obscure, such as undersigned or yours truly. (See also **Gobbledygook**)

On; upon. Both words have the same meaning, but by and large *on* denotes rest, and *upon* indicates action—though *on* can serve practically in all cases.

>The paint *on* the wall is wet.
>This is a new book *on* the life of Mahatma Gandhi.
>He jumped *on* the thief and overpowered him.
>He jumped *upon* the thief and overpowered him.

One of . . . This phrase is followed by a plural noun and a singular verb because it means 'one of the several named things or persons' and the operative word is the singular 'one'.

>One of the *teachers* has a PhD. [*Not:* one of the *teacher* has a PhD]
>One of my *books* was stolen. [*Not:* one of my *book* was stolen]

Onomatopoeia is a figure of speech in which words are formed which imitate or echo the sounds that suggest the object or action that they refer to. They are used for rhetorical effect.

>The bees were *buzzing* around the flowers.
>The cobra *hissed* at the farmer.
>The cuckoo was *cooing* in the garden.
>The *sizzling* of meat in the pan enhanced my appetite.
>I lost my wallet in the *hurly-burly* of the football match.
>The cat was trapped in a high branch of the tree and was *mewing* pathetically

Opposite means 'facing each other' or 'contrary in position or kind'. By itself it can be used thus:

My house is *opposite* the Hanuman temple.
Opposite ends of the road are now barred.

The construction when opposite takes 'to' as in:
My house is opposite *to* the Hanuman temple
is grammatically correct but the usage is becoming obsolete.

Ordinal Numbers. An ordinal number is a number defining a thing's position in a series and is spelt out in full (like *first*, *second*, and so on):
Eighteenth century
Second order yellow
Twelfth line
Seventieth anniversary

Orphan and **widow** are nouns that have a very special connotation in typing and printing. *Orphan* is the first line of a paragraph that is set as the last line on a page or column, cut off from the rest of the paragraph on the next page. *Widow* is a last word or short line of a paragraph falling at the top of a page or column of the text, separated from its related text on the previous page or column. While preparing a typescript care should be taken to avoid such *orphans* and *widows*.

Outward; outwards. It is sometimes a problem to decide which of the two words is appropriate in a particular situation. It should be remembered that *outward* means 'on, of, or from outside'; and *outwards* means 'moving towards the outside direction or away from the centre'.
The *outward* appearance of the car is good.
The spines radiate *outwards* from the body of a hedgehog.

Oxymoron is a figure of speech where contradictory words are combined in an expression.
The hanging of Bhagat Singh was *legal murder* by the British.
The new township is nothing but a *concrete jungle*.
His absurd proposals were greeted by a *deafening silence*.
He is a typical bureaucrat, he *makes haste slowly*.

Palindrome is a word, phrase, or number that reads the same backwards as well as forwards. Such a word is only a literary curiosity.
> Dial — Laid
> Madam — Madam
> Malayalam—Malayalam
> Not a ton — Not a ton
> 1881 — 1881
> Dog as a devil deified—deified lived as a god
> Able was I ere I saw Elba—able was I ere I was able

Paradox is a figure of speech in which an apparently absurd or self-contradictory statement is made that may in fact be true.
> Mahatma Gandhi's tenet of *ahimsa* and exhortation not to bear injustice is a paradox because if you fight injustice there is bound to be some conflict.
> His outward humility hides a ruthless tyrant.

Partial; partly; partially. *Partial* is an adjective, while the other two words are adverbs. *Partial* denotes 'not total' or 'incomplete', as also 'biased in favour of one side'. *Partly* means 'to some extent' or 'not completely'; and partially has the meaning of 'incompletely'.
> She has regained *partial* movement of her arm after physiotherapy.
> He is *partial* to his daughter because of her disability.
> The devise is made *partly* of steel and *partly* of engineering plastic.
> She became *partially* blind after the accident.

Parts of Speech. See **Grammar**.

Pathetic fallacy is a figure of speech in which words are assigned human feelings or traits to inanimate objects. Though such words may look incongruous, they admirably convey the meaning intended. [also see **personification**]
> The *cruel* tsunami claimed thousands of life when it struck the Tamil Nadu coast.
> The *angry* sea around the Cape of Storms claims the life of many sailors every year.
> The VIP colony *enjoys* uninterrupted electric supply when rest of the city is plunged in darkness.
> The dilapidated monuments in Lucknow are *crying* for restoration.

Percent. The British use two words, *per cent*, which is logical grammar to mean 'each hundred', but the Americans make it into a single word. This is obviously a practical style and should be the acceptable form because the nouns *percentage* and *percentile* are easily formed from it.

Persian words used in English are not many. Most of those that are included in English vocabulary have come indirectly from Hindustani (Hindi and Urdu), such as bazaar, shikar, sepoy, caravan, jungle, pajama, veranda, and so on. Some that have been absorbed completely are: algorithm, candy, jargon, magic, paradise, sugar, tapestry, tiara, tiger and cow.

Perhaps; Probable; Possible. There is often confusion about the correct use of these words as each has a different sense. *Perhaps* (adverb) means 'maybe', that is something open to doubt, uncertainty or conjecture. *Probable* (adjective) means 'that may be expected or likely to happen'; from it *probably* (adverb) meaning 'most likely to happen'. *Possible* (adjective) has the meaning of 'that can happen or be done', and from it *possibly* (adverb) meaning 'perhaps' and *possibility* (noun) meaning 'what is possible'.

> I don't know but *perhaps* I may have to go to Delhi this weekend.
> The *probable* cause of his death was heart failure.
> *Probably* he died of heart failure.
> It is *possible* that the jail staff helped the prisoner to escape.
> The escape of the prisoners was *possibly* an inside job.
> The *possibility* of the jail staff helping the prisoner to escape cannot be ruled out.

Parody is a literary work in which the style of an author or work is closely imitated for comic effect or in ridicule.

Person; personnel; persona. *Person* is an 'individual human being', while *personnel* refers to 'a body of people employed in an organization'; *persona* is an image or personality that a person projects in public.

> He is a *person* who is revered for his intellectual attainments.
> The *personnel* in this department are well-trained sales people.
> His *persona* in public is that of a man who has dedicated himself to serve humanity.

Personal pronouns. The order in any sequence of personal pronouns should be as follows: second person third person first person. it's popular as 321.

> Your wife, his wife and my wife will go in the same car. [Not: my wife…]
> My wife and I went to the evening show of the movie. [Not: I and my wife…}
> This concession means a lot to you and me. [Not: me and you]

Personification is a figure of speech where a thing or object is attributed a quality as if it were a person or has human form. Its proper use in prose can enliven any text. [Compare with **Pathetic fallacy**]

> The first monsoon showers *bathed the earth* with fragrance.
> When I woke up in the morning I found the *sun smiling* through the open window.

The *wind was howling* throughout the cruel night.
The *moon was playing* peek-a-boo with clouds that wintry night.

Phenomena is actually the plural of 'phenomenon', but is often used as a singular in speech and writing, which is a mistake.
>Aurora borealis is a light *phenomenon*.
>There are several *phenomena* of light that can be seen in the southern sky.

Phrase. It is a small group of words usually without a predicate. It forms a grammatical unit but not a sentence. [It is different from a **Clause**.]
>See below.
>A beautiful watch

Pidgin English is to be distinguished from **Hinglish.** *Pidgin English* is a grammatically simplified language used for communication between English-speaking and people speaking a different language. Actually, the term is applied to the Creole language which evolved from pidginised French that is spoken by blacks in southern Louisiana, USA. There is no pidgin English as such in India, but some phrases like the following that one comes across often in India could be so classed. In such cases special meaning has been accorded to an English word.
>*Accidental car* = for a car that has been damaged in an accident or otherwise
>*Accountable Manager* = Accounts Manager
>*Time-pass* = passing time

Platitude is a figure of speech where an overused banal, trite or stale remark or statement is used. It is best avoided in speech and writing though its use is quite common.
>Ha! He is neither wise nor otherwise!
>The teacher kept on urging the students to speak the truth always.
>The politician assured the public that he will build new roads, schools and hospitals if elected.

Plurals are generally formed by putting a suffix 's' or 'es' after a noun, but there are many nouns which do not subscribe to this rule and have entirely different words. Some common examples such irregular plurals are given here:

<u>Singular</u>	<u>Plural</u>
Foot	feet
Man	men
Mouse	mice
tooth	teeth

Plurals of Foreign Words. There are several words from Latin (L) and Greek (G) which are now part of the English vocabulary and generally follow the original style of plural making, though some are also pluralised by suffixing 's' or 'es' according to the usual English usage.

Singular	Plural
Addendum (L)	Addenda
Alumna (L)	alumnae
Alumnus (L)	alumni
Appendix (L)	Appendices / Appendixes
Bacterium (L)	Bacteria
Cactus (L)	cacti
Corrigendum (L)	Corrigenda
Cranium (G)	Crania / craniums
Criterion (G)	Criteria
Curriculum (L)	Curricula / curriculums
Erratum (L)	Errata
Focus (L)	Foci / Focuses
Fungus (L)	Fungi / Funguses
Genus (L)	Genera
Gladiolus (L)	Gladioli
Honorarium (L)	Honoraria / honorariums
Index (L)	Indices / indexes
Medium (L)	Media / mediums
Memorandum (L)	Memoranda / Memorandums
Ovum (L)	Ova
Plateau (F)	Plateaux / plateaus
Premium (L)	Premiums
Rectum (L)	Recta / rectums
Spectrum (L)	Spectra / spectrums
Stratum (L)	Strata
Syllabus (L)	Syllabi / syllabuses
Thorax (G)	Thoraces / thoraxes

Plurals of in-laws. The making of plurals of the relationships causes quite some confusion The rule is that the plural goes to the main relation.

sons-in-law [Not, son-in-laws]
daughters-in-law
mothers-in-law
fathers-in-law

However, plural 'in-laws' can be used correctly for parents and close relatives of husband/wife in certain contexts as exemplified below:

Her *in-laws* were quite supportive when she decided to take up a job.

Plurals of compound official ranks. A common mistake in making plurals of some multiword official ranks and designations is by adding 's' at the end of the compound designation. Such designations are of two parts—the noun which is the basic designation, and its qualifier adjective. Only the noun can be pluralized and not the qualifier (which itself may be a noun). The basic rule here is to pluralize the basic designation: The examples given here will make it clear. The given rule is that the noun part of the designation is pluralized. Let's consider the rank *Directors General*—here the basic rank is 'director' (noun) so it is pluralized. But in *Major Generals* the basic rank is 'general' (noun) so it is pluralized. [The term *Director Generals* is often encountered, but it is wrong.]

> Assistant Advocates General
> Deputy Directors General
> Editors-in-Chief
> Governors General
> Lieutenant Colonels
> Major Generals
> Poets Laureate
> Postmasters General
> Rear Admirals
> Sergeants-at-Arms [*Sergeant* is a noun to qualify *arms*]

However, abbreviations are pluraled as usual:

> DGs
> DDGs
> PMGs
> AAGs

Plurals and Singulars the same. Some nouns have the same word as plural, like the following, but a few also pluralise by adding the usual 's'.:

<u>Singular</u>	<u>Plural</u>
deer	deer
fish	fish(es)
sheep	sheep

Poetry is one of the two genres of writing and literature together with **Prose**. Poetry is metrical writing and includes a *poem* which is a composition in verse that is arranged in lines and has regular rhythm and often rhyme where imagery is used; there are several other styles also. Writers of poetry pieces often take liberties with grammar, sentence construction and spelling. It is opposed to **Prose** which is the ordinary form of spoken and written language. Poetry takes several forms. *Verse* is a group of lines that form a unit in a poem or song arranged with a metrical rhythm (but a *blank verse* may not use rhyme). *Rhyme* is when there is correspondence of sound between endings of words in lines in a poem. *Ode* is a lyrical poem typically praising or glorifying some one or something. On the other hand, *dirge* is a mournful song. *Hymn* is a religious song praising God. *Ballad* is a popular poem or song that can be sung. *Sonnet* is a poem of fourteen lines using several rhyme schemes. *Haiku* is a poem of seventeen syllables in three lines adopted from the Japanese. *Nursery rhyme* is a light-hearted poem which children learn. *Limerick* is a humorous five-line poem. *Doggerel* is a slipshod or unpoetic verse often for comical affect. *Ditty* is a short song often used in advertising. There are also some other terms associated with poetry. *Lyrics* are words of a song or poems expressing emotions. *Poesy* is a term for sentimental poetic writing or the art of poetry. *Jingle* is a short verse or song marked by a catchy phraseology, often used in advertisements.

> In ancient times there were court bards whose job was to compose and sing *odes* and *ballads* in praise of their masters.
> Keats's *Ode to a Nightingale* has been included in Class XII textbook.
> Shakespeare's love *sonnets* are some of the best in English literature.
> William Wordsworth's *poem* 'The Rainbow' has been included in the class X textbook.
> John Keats *poetry* is full of imagery and describes the beauty of nature.
> Vikram Seth's novel 'the Golden Gate' is entirely written in *verse*.
> The best known *rhyme* is 'Twinkle twinkle little star....' that we learnt early in our lives.
> Similarly, the best known *nursery rhyme* is 'Jack and Jill went up the hill....'

Portmanteau words are formed by blending the sounds and combining the meanings of two words. Some examples:

> Avionics [*avi*ation + electr*onics*]
> Brunch [*br*eakfast + l*unch*]
> Internet [*inter*national + *net*work]
> Motel [*mo*tor + ho*tel*]
> Netizen [Inter*net* + citi*zen*]
> Sensex [*Sens*itive + ind*ex*]
> Smog [*sm*oke + f*og*]

Portuguese words. Goa was a Portuguese colony for a long time and the Portuguese influence is still evident there. Some words from Portuguese have filtered down to us. Fruits like *banana, cashew, guava,* and *mango* have come from Portuguese but through Indian languages. India got *monsoon* from Portuguese which in turn took it from Arabic. Other words from Portuguese are *cobra, marmalade* and *pagoda*. A Portuguese word often heard is *palaver*, meaning 'long and tedious discussion'. A military unit trained and organised as shock troops is *commando*, also from the Portuguese.

Practice; practise. These two words sounding the same are very confusing as the British and American usages differ. We consider here that *practice* is a noun and *practise* is a verb.

> The doctor has a good *practice* in the town
> The doctor *practises* in the town

Prepone as the antonym of 'postpone' is widely used in India, but cannot be found in most dictionaries. It seems quite reasonable that if 'post-' as a prefix means 'subsequent' or 'later', the prefix 'pre-' having the opposite meaning of 'before' or 'prior too should be accepted. Let us examine the incongruity: 'postpone' is made from the French, *post + ponere,* and in 'prepone' only the prefix is substituted, and so the word appears to be a legitimate creation. This Indian contribution to vocabulary has now been gracefully accepted at last by the Oxford English Dictionary and has been made a part of standard English like so many other Indian words.

Productive; productivity. Both the words have their root in 'production', but have different connotations. *Productive* indicates the ability of someone to produce large amounts of something, while *productivity* refers to someone's ability or effectiveness to produce something.

> The work she was doing was quite *productive* as it benefited the community but after a heart attack she could not devote enough time and naturally the *productivity* fell down.
>
> It was a highly *productive* endeavour churning out a variety of goods but after the death of Mr. Sinha his son could not manage the company properly and its *productivity* fell down drastically..

Pronoun dilemma. The standard grammatical construction is that a singular noun takes a singular pronoun. The problem arises as to which gender pronoun to use after a neutral noun. In a sentence like this: "The viewer was asked to indicate his or her preference." most writers tend to use only the masculine 'his'. But the viewer could as well be a woman. So, some grammar conscious writer may frame the sentence like this: "The viewer *was* asked to indicate *his/her* preference." This obviously is a very stilted sentence and the present practice is to use 'they' in place of 'he/she'. Now, the sentence would read thus: "The viewer *was* asked to indicate *their* preference." This usage is perfectly acceptable in modern prose. Not only in modern writing or speech, even several classical authors have used this construction in which the singular noun takes the plural 'they'.

Proper nouns as words. See **Words from proper nouns.**

Prose is the ordinary form of spoken and written language which is the general form of spoken and written language. This work is mainly concerned with this form of the English language.

Proverb / maxim / adage / saying are synonyms. Either word means a short, pithy popular statement that is in general used to illustrate a point or situation. It is effectively used to state a general truth in all types of writing or verbal communication. Sayings, used judiciously, serve to illustrate or emphasise your points and views. There are hundreds of proverbs that are in frequent use and there are numerous compilations available in the market for your use. (See also **Aphorism**)

>Better to reign in hell than serve in heaven. (Milton)
>To err is human, to forgive divine. (Pope)
>There is honour among thieves.

Proximo. See **Instant...**

Pull as a verb that signifies movement towards something; its past and past participle is the same **pulled**. Verbal phrases formed from *pull* have different meanings.

>In the village he has two bullocks to *pull* his cart.

pull apart means 'dismember' or 'separate'
>The two factions of the party *pulled apart* on the support of the Women's Reservation Bill.

pull away means 'to withdraw':
>At the last moment, she *pulled away* from the decision to marry him.

pull back means 'to withdraw from something'
>The army column *pulled back* in time from the ambush.

pull down means 'demolish something'
>The municipal authorities decided to *pull down* the unauthorized structures.

pull off means 'to achieve or accomplish something despite difficulties'
>The merger of the two companies was *pulled off* by adroit handling of the two boards by Mr.Sinha.

pull out means 'withdraw from undertaking' or 'extract'.
>The dentist *pulled out* her troublesome tooth.
>The army *pulled out* from peace-keeping task in the Sudan because of non-cooperation by the local authorities.

pull through means 'to recover from some dangerous or difficult situation'
>The company *pulled through* the stock market crash by drastically cutting back the work-force.

pull together means 'to cooperate in a task'
>If the employees and management of the company don't *pull together* it will go into liquidation.

pull up means 'to stop or halt something'
>He was *pulled up* by the manger for his poor sales record.

Pun is a play on words or humorous use of words so as to convey a double meaning or the meaning of another word. Although a pun is dubbed as "the lowest form of humour" it is delightful and attracts reader's attention and interest. Pun is widespread—one can find puns everyday in newspapers and magazines, in headlines and elsewhere. Shakespeare said that 'Brevity is the soul of wit' and it is largely true. However, puns should be used judiciously in serious, professional and official writing. A well-known example is provided by the author Hilaire Bellock's couplet:

> When I am dead, I hope it may be said
> His sins were scarlet, but his books were read.

There is no end to examples but just a few here:

> A cat has claws at the end of its paws but a comma is a pause at the end of a clause.
> The affluenza epidemic that has spread among the young call centre employees has given a great fillip to consumerism.
> Outdoor spelling bee contest was called off because of bad spell of weather.
> Cardiac surgeon Dr. Devi Shetty has heart-warming concern for the poor.
> Health apparatus in U.P. needs nursing
> Your arguments are sound—nothing but sound.
> Sugar mill disinvestment is not so sweet.
> An epitaph on a lawyer's grave: 'He lied throughout his life and now lies still'.

Punctuations. These are devices in written or printed matter to clarify meaning natural to speech by influencing sentence structure to enhance readability by employing standard marks or signs. The following are the generally used marks:

.	Period/full stop/dot
,	Comma
;	Semicolon
:	Colon
'	Apostrophe
' '	Single inverted commas/quotation marks
" "	Double inverted commas/quotation marks
?	Question mark
!	Exclamation mark
/	Slash/solidus/virgule
-	Hyphen
—	Dash, em
–	Dash, en
( )	Parentheses
[ ]	Square brackets
{ }	Curly brackets/braces

Some marks are exclusive to computers:

\	Back slash
_	Underscore

Put is a verb which essentially means 'to move something to particular place' or 'to express in words'; also **putting**. Its past and past participle are the same **put**. Verbal phrases formed from *put* have different meanings.

> She *put* her book inside her bag and then forgot all about it.
> She *put* her ideas about the Women's Bill in an article published last Tuesday.

put across means 'to convey'.
> She *put across* her views so forcefully that the boss had to agree with her.

put aside means 'to set aside'.
> *Putting aside* the objections of her family she married her boy friend.

put away means 'to save'.
> She *put away* most of her saving in government bonds.

put back means 'to defer'.
> The proposal to construct a new toilet was *put back* for future consideration.

put down means 'to record' or 'to suppress'.
> To make sure of its implication the proposal was *put down* in writing.
> The rebellion was *put down* with ruthlessness.

put forward means 'to submit' or 'to suggest'.
> The theory *put forward* by the police that she was killed by her father is absurd.

put in means 'to enter'.
> She *put in* a word of praise for her junior to the boss.

put off means 'to postpone'.
> The decision to have a new principal has been *put off* for the time being.

put on means 'to add' or 'to perform'.
> She has *put on* a lot of weight after the birth of her baby.
> A play on Mangal Pandey was *put on* during the centenary celebration of 1857 uprising.

put out means 'to extinguish' or 'to announce'.
> The fire was *put out* by the fire tenders in about two hours.
> A notice was *put out* that the school will start from 7 a.m. from Monday.

put through means 'to execute'.
> The new government has *put through* a number of reforms in the power sector.

put up means 'to offer'.
> The authorities have *put up* the property for sale for non-payment of taxes.

put up with means 'to endure'.
> She could no loner *put up with* the torture and applied for divorce.

Range, Expression of. There are two ways to express a range of dates, distances, etc.

'From' requires 'to'; and 'between' goes with 'and'. The correct usage is as follows:
> I was in the United States *from* 1978 *to* 1986.
> I was in the Unites States *between* 1978 *and* 1986.
> The distance *from* Lucknow *to* Kanpur is 86 km.
> The distance *between* Lucknow *and* Kanpur is 86 km.

It is wrong to pair 'between' and 'to' as in the following examples:
> I was in the United States *between* 1978 *to* 1986.
> The distance *between* Lucknow *to* Kanpur is 86 km.

Rational, rationale. While *rational* is an adjective meaning 'based on reason and logic', *rationale* is a noun which means 'reasons or logical basis for a course of belief or action'.
> It is not at all *rational* to impose this tax as computers are educational tools.
> The *rationale* for imposing this restriction is to prevent smuggling across the border.

Recession', depression. These are terms in economics which indicate decline in economic activities. *Recession* is a term used to describe a period of decline in economic activity in which trade and industrial activity are reduced. This leads to *depression* which is a period of severe low in general economic activity and is marked by rising unemployment.
> After its war in Iraq the U.S. economy is heading towards *recession*.
> The Great *depression* of 1929 and subsequent years caused such a financial and industrial slump in the U.S. from which it could recover after great effort.

Red besides being a very conspicuous colour is indicative of danger. In public view, capitalized Red largely refers to communists or their fellow travellers.
> The *Red* brigade of Communist Party terrorised the people of Nandigram in West Bengal.
> The *Reds* are opposed to any cooperation with America.

Refute; repudiate. *Refute* means 'to prove something wrong or false'. *Repudiate* means 'to reject as false or unjust'.
> He *refuted* the allegation that he was present at the accident site by producing the attendance register of the factory where he worked.

The ancient belief that the sun revolved around the earth was *repudiated* by Copernicus in the 16th century.

Relation; relative. In the meaning of 'kinsmen/kinswomen' these nouns can both be used as synonyms.

Repartee is a quick, witty reply or comment or interchange of words which is a mode of expression intended to arouse amusement.

> Doctor: You have lived to be an old man.
> Patient: Because I never employed you as my physician.

Respect; respective. It appears at the first glance that the second word is a derivative of the noun *respect* meaning 'esteem', it is actually derived from the verbal meaning of 'reference to' or 'relation to'. *Respective* is an adjective having the meaning of 'in the given order', and *respectively* is formed from it to mean 'in order already mentioned'.

> With *respect* to your invitation, I am sorry but I cannot come.
> The two are heads of their *respective* branches.
> Ramesh and Kamesh are heads of the sales and purchase departments, *respectively*.
> [A comma is used before *respectively*.]

Rest; restive. These two similar looking words have almost opposing meanings. While the verb *rest* means 'cease from exertion or action' the adjective *restive* denotes the opposite condition of restless, meaning 'unruly' or 'fretful'.

> The doctor has advised her a week's *rest*.
> The audience became *restive* when the play was delayed by an hour.

Revolve; rotate. These two verbs describing motion are likely to be confused. *Revolve* means 'to move in a circular path or turn around a central axis', while *rotate* has the meaning of 'to turn about a centre or axis'. These two words are often used to describe the motion of celestial bodies, like the planets, particularly the Earth.

> The Earth *revolves* around the sun in about 365 days, and *rotates* on its axis in about 24 hours.
> Her life *revolves* around her son since his birth.
> The farmers in the district earn good money by *rotating* their crops.

Rhetoric. Speech or written language designed to impress. This is a skill in effective writing or speaking that is likely to impress and may be inflated or exaggerated language.

Roman numerals. See **Numerals, Roman.**

Russian words. Several Russian words have recently found general use in English writing. A few common ones are noted here.

Commissar = Some one who attempts to control public opinion (after a Communist official who was assigned to control party loyalty)
> The *commissars* of the CP(M) have not succeeded in taming the people of Nandigram.

Glasnost = Practice of open government [adopted from the former Soviet policy permitting open discussion of political or social issues before breakup of the USSR]
> *Glasnost* became a regular feature after independence in the former republics of the Soviet Union.

Gulag = A harsh penal system of USSR consisting of labour camps. (applied to any such camp anywhere)
> Some autocratic regimes in Africa have created *gulags* in their countries to oppress their opponents.

Perestroka = The reform of political and economic systems initiated before the breakup of the Soviet Union.
> *Perestroka* has brought enormous changes in the erstwhile Soviet republics.

Pogrom = An organized massacre of hapless people.
> The *pogrom* followed by the Nazi's killed tens of thousand of Jews.

Politburo = Principal policymaking and executive committee of a Communist party
> The CP(M) *Politburo* in Kerala has decided to suspend four members for indiscipline.

Steppe = A large area of unforested grassland.
> There are several large areas of *steppe* in central United States.

Tsar, Czar = A person of great power (from the all-powerful emperors of Russia).
> Azim Premji is the Czar of the Wipro empire.

Sarcasm is a figure of speech in which satirical or bitingly ironic expression is used to make fun of somebody.

> Sure! He is wise—but with the prefix 'other'.
> Your explanation is as clear as mud.
> The slogan of the politician 'garibi hatao' is very apt as they are busy in their personal 'garibi hatao' movement!
> Yes, I know. He is a great musician: he knows how to play a radio and tape-recorder!

Satire is the use of humour, irony, exaggeration, **sarcasm**, or ridicule to expose and criticize or discredit people's follies, vices or stupidity. For example, George Orwell's *Animal Farm* is a satire on extremism practiced by Stalin during the Russian Revolution.

Saying. See **Proverb…**

Saw. See **Proverb…**

Semi-, hemi-, quasi-, demi-, all these prefixes mean 'half', but are used with different senses. Though *semi-* means exactly half (semi-monthly), it also means 'partially' (semi-precious, semi-civilised). *Hemi-* is 'half, (hemisphere), and also 'not complete' (hemimorphic, hemicycle). *Quasi-* gives a sense of approximate or almost (quasi-judicial). *Demi* is half or partial (demigod; demiword). Note the use or omission of the hyphen.

Set as a verb essentially means 'to put'. Its past and past participle forms are the same **set**. Verbal phrases formed from *set* have different meanings.

> The time of the wedding was *set* at 10.35 p.m. by the pundits.
> The child was *set* free after a huge ransom was paid to the abductors.
> The alarm has been *set* to go off at 5 a.m.
> His broken arm has been *set* by the doctor with a splint.

set about means 'to start with determination'.
> After moving into a new house she *set about* decorating it.

set against means roughly 'to oppose'
> In the property dispute the two brothers were *set against* each other.

set apart means 'to put aside or separate'.
> She has *set apart* rupees five lakhs for the wedding of her daughter.

set aside means 'to lay aside' or 'to reverse or repudiate'.
: The Supreme Court has *set aside* the lower court's judgment.

set back means 'to delay or impede'.
: The new rules *set back* the plans of the company to build a new mall.

set forth means 'to begin a journey' or 'to describe in writing'.
: The pilgrims *set forth* on their journey after a dip in the Ganga.
: Everything has been *set forth* in the prospectus by the university.

set off means 'to depart', or 'to explode'.
: The team *set off* for the peak soon after reaching the base camp.
: The bombs were *set off* one after the other within the space of a few minutes.

set on (upon) means 'to attack'.
: The crowd caught the chain-snatcher and *set on (upon)* him with sticks.

set out means 'to begin or start'.
: She *set out* to start the new venture but there were so many obstacles that she quit.

set up means 'to arrange or build'.
: After getting her degree she *set up* a clinic in her house.

Several; various. Some people use these two words as synonymous, but these two adjectives have different meanings. *Several* connotes 'more than two', while *various* implies 'different kinds' or 'unlike'.

Several judgments of the court have accepted the legality of this law.

Various judgments of the court have given different interpretations of the law.

Shall; will; should; would. The proper usage between these verbs is quite complex, but here attempt has been made to simply usage. *Shall* is ordinarily used in the fist person and *will* in the second and third. *I* and *we* take 'should' and *he, she, it, they,* etc., take 'would'.:
: I *shall* go home.
: You *will* go home.
: He *will* go home.
: I *should* go home.
: He *should* go home.
: She *would* not go home.
: They *would* not go home
: It *would* not be right to turn him out.
: She *would* not go home after the class.

But *will* in the first person is commonly used in place of *shall*. It can also be used to show determination:
: We *will* go home now.
: I *will* go home. [I am determined to go home.]

Will is always implied in a contraction:
> *I'll* go home now.
> *We'll* go home now.
> *You'll* go home now.

Shall in the second and third person indicates an order:
> You *shall* go home. [You must go home.]
> He *shall* go home. [He must go home.]

Should is subjunctive of *shall*, and *would* is subjunctive of past of *will*:
> My mother said that I *should* be home before midnight.
> You *should* be thankful for the research grant given to you.
> I *would* like to help you but I have no money now.
> We knew that he *would* not be able to stand the strain.

Shambles meaning 'chaotic' or 'badly disorganised' appears like a plural but is actually a singular noun and is used with 'a' before it.
> His house was in *a shambles* after it was hit by the storm.

Shopping; marketing. These are two opposite activities though relating to one object: *shopping* involves 'buying' or 'purchasing', while marketing involves 'selling'.
> She went *shopping* to the nearest supermarket to buy groceries.
> He *markets* the vegetables from his farm to a wholesaler in the nearby town.

Shore; bank. Both the words mean 'land that adjoins a water body', but the usage is different. Take care: *shore* is of ocean, sea or lake, but *bank* is that of river or stream.
> *Shore* of the Atlantic
> Bay of Bengal
> *Shore* along the Vamband Lake
> *Banks* along the Ganga River

Shortened Forms are a few letters taken out from longer words to form independent words in the meaning of the longer ones. Some popular examples:

ad	...	*ad*vertisement
bra	...	*bra*ssiere
exam	...	*exam*ination
flue	...	in*flue*nza
lab	...	*lab*oratory
maths	...	*math*ematics
memo	...	*memo*randum
rail	...	*rail*way/*rail*road
Xmas	...	Christmas [X stands for Christ]

[sic]. When some readers encounter this word within square brackets (sometimes within parentheses) they are sometimes mystified as to what this means. It means 'just as, so, thus' from the Latin *sicut* and is inserted after a preceding printed word or phrase to indicate that the apparent word (often a mistake) is printed or reproduced exactly as the original in a quote. Such a word or phrase may be incorrect and the writer quoting it wants to make it clear that he is not responsible for the mistake. In the example below the correct word should have been 'pudding'.

>He said that the *padding* [sic] served at the meal was not fresh. [pudding]

Sight; vision. These two nouns essentially mean 'the power or faculty of seeing'. The word *sight* is generally used in this meaning (ignoring the attribute of a person or thing having an unattractive appearance). In the larger context *vision* also indicates a mental image of something imagined or planned for the future.

>Even at this ripe old age her eye *sight* is perfect
>He lost the *sight/vision* in his right eye after an accident.
>Even at this ripe old age the *vision* in both her eyes is perfect.
>The *vision* of the founding father of independent India was to make it a great nation.

Simile is a figure of speech in which a comparison is made pointing out a similarity between things or persons otherwise unlike. Words 'like' or 'as' are used in the sentences.

>His house was lit up *like a Charismas tree*.
>It collapsed *as a pack of cards*.
>At the New Year party he *drank like a fish*.
>At eighty he is *fit as a fiddle*.
>His assurance is *as good as gold*.
>He hates him *like poison*.
>His new quilt is *light as a feather*.
>His mind is *sharp as a razor*.
>The two friends are *thick as thieves*.
>What you say is *clear* as mud

Since; from. *Since* is used to denote a point of time and comes after a verb in the present perfect tense and can be used only in reference to the past. *From* may be used with any form of tense, past, present, and future.

>He has been absent *since* last Monday.
>She *began* her dance lesson *from* yesterday.
>She *begins her* dance *lesson* from today.
>She will *begin her* dance lessons *from* tomorrow.

Singular and plural. A common mistake found in some Indian writing is the use of plural verb with a singular noun and vice versa. Another not uncommon mistake is the use of a noun in its plural but its pronoun in singular, or the other way round, in the same sentence, and singular and plural forms in different sentences of the same paragraph or write-up. Just a little care can obviate such mistakes.

Slang. These are words and phrases that are in informal use, often abusive or insulting. They are commonly used in speech, and should be avoided in good prose though they could be used for picturesque expression. There are hundreds and there is even a dictionary devoted to them. Here are a few heard recently.

> The *old geezer* [old man] is very tight with his *dough* [money].
> The *dude* [man] has fancy *threads* [clothes].
> The *blighter* [person] has not shown up since he borrowed a thousand from me.
> I asked him to shut his *trap* [mouth] after he had *babbled* [talked incoherently] for long.

Slang words for people. Often slang words are used for people or groups of people—some pejoratively—which are in common parlance. A few selected examples are given here.

Slang	Normal
Aussie	Australian
Brits	British
Chinks	Chinese
Commies	communists
Gujju	Gujarati
Oz	Australian
Paki	Pakistani
Prez	President
Veep	Vice-president

SMS language has come into extensive use by mobile phone users. SMS is the abbreviation of *Short Messaging Service*. This form is inappropriate in formal writing and should be shunned.

Gr8	=	great
B4	=	before
UC	=	you see
Un42n8	=	unfortunate
10denC	=	tendency
thanQ	=	thank you
URinYted	=	you are invited

Sobriquet or Nickname. A descriptive name substituted for a person's or thing's proper name. (Compare with **Euphuism**)

> *Pink city* = Jaipur (Rajasthan)
> *Roof of the World* = The Pamir Mountain

Deshbandhu = C. F. Andrews
Qaid-e-Azam = Mohammad Ali Jinnah

Social; sociable. These two adjectives have somewhat different connotations. *Social* has the meaning of 'relating to society', while sociable has the element of friendliness in it.

> Man is a *social* animal.
> Her *social* circle is confined to her colleagues only.
> The new member is very *sociable* and makes friends easily.
> The judges cannot afford to be very *sociable* because they must ensure their independence.

Solecism is flagrant offence against grammar, idiom or etiquette. The word is after the people of Soloi, a town in ancient Cilicia (in south Turkey), whose people spoke a dialect which was considered unattractive or incorrect.

South is not only a direction on the compass but in current parlance it has acquired other connotations as well. It has now also come to mean 'Developing nations of the world', also sometimes called the 'Third World' which comprise a group of nations, especially in Africa and Asia, not aligned with either the Communist or the non-Communist blocks. It also means 'a state of decline or ruin'. 'South' has also acquired the meaning of 'lower' or 'diminishing' in the language of economics and the adverb formed from it. The expression *south paw* means 'left-hander' person. [See also the entry below]

> The *South* has still to reach the infrastructure development which is already there in the Western countries.
> After strong fiscal measures the prices of commodities had started stabilising but the recent increase in oil prices has caused the economy to go *south*.

Southward; southwards; southerly; southern. The correct use of the first two words is rather confusing. *Southward* is adjective and adverb both, meaning 'in a southerly direction' and *southwards* is adverb only meaning 'towards the south'. Since the sense is the same, either can be used. *Southerly* has the meaning of 'in a southward position or direction' Southern means 'situated towards or facing the south'.

> The *southward* trek brought them to a pond with crystal clear water.
> Moving *southwards* they came upon the carcass of a tiger killed by poachers.
> The *southerly* wind brought the monsoon showers.
> The *southern* suburb of the town is practically a slum.

Spanish words. There are several words from the Spanish language that are in current use in English. A few are given here.

Aficionado = a person very knowledgeable and enthusiastic about a subject or activity

> He is an *aficionado* of contract bridge and plays daily at the club.

Barbeque = structure for grilling food, and the food produced there from
   The food was prepared on a *barbeque* is very delicious.

Cargo = goods carried commercially on a ship, aircraft or truck
   The *cargo* is generally carried in containers.

Embargo = official suspension of trade or commerce with a particular country
   An *embargo* has been clamped on arms shipment to the LTTE.

Guerilla = a member of a small independent group taking part in a irregular warfare
   The Maoist *guerillas* killed several policemen in Jharkhand.

Junta = a political or military clique ruling a country by force
   The *junta* in Burma has arrested a large number of monks.

Peccadillo = a venial sin, fault or offence.
   The *peccadilloes* of the rich brats in town has come for a lots of criticism.

Peon = a menial or a person of low rank.
   Every officer in India has at least one peon in his office.

Siesta = mid-day or any other rest
   A *siesta* in the afternoon is recommended for the elderly.

Specially; especially. These two adverbs are quite confusing to use. *Specially* means 'of or for a particular purpose, occasion, thing or person'. *Especially* introduces an element of intensity.
   The dress was made *specially* for the Indian team.
   He dressed *specially* for attending the party.
   The trophy was designed *specially* for the World Cup.
   The function was organized *specially* to honour the winning team.
   The new chair has been designed *especially* for the physically challenged.
   The new boss *especially* doesn't like people who smoke in the office.

Spelling. Correct spelling of words is essential in any writing, but spelling of some words used may differ in different countries; this difference is marked in some words particularly between the British and United States styles. Some derivative words may also have two different forms of spelling. [In this connection see also **-ise** or **-ize**]

Spoonerism is accidental or deliberate transposition of the sound of initial letters of two words in a spoken sentence. The word is derived from the name of an English educator, W.A. Spooner, who was prone to such speech.
   You have *hissed* my *mystery* lecture. (You have missed my history lecture.)
   You have *tasted* two *werms* this year. (You have wasted two terms this year.)

Subjunctive mood. It is a mood relating to a verb form that represents something that is highly unlikely or contrary to facts, that is, it a way to express a wish. In this mood the verb 'were' is used instead of 'was' even for a singular noun.

> I wish I *were* as rich as the Ambanis.
> If only I could fly I *would* go immediately to America to help my son.

Substantial; substantive. These two adjectives are closely related and may be used as synonyms in some cases. In finer distinction, *substantial* has the meaning of 'ample', while *substantive* means 'not subsidiary, having separate existence'.

> The *substantial/substantive* increase in the wages was welcomed by the staff.
> The new manager has made *substantial* increase in the wages.
> The poor were fed a *substantial* menu of rice, dal and vegetables.
> The union leaders had *substantive* talks with the management to avoid the strike.

Summary. A document often requires a condensation for ease of study, information in a nutshell, etc. *Précis* is a concise summary of essential points of a paragraph, a passage, or even a chapter often required for perusal by others. A scientific or technical communication often requires a brief summary, called the *Abstract,* at the beginning of the paper or separately which gives the salient points discussed in the communication to enable the reader to judge whether he needs to peruse the whole document. *Condensation* is compression of a piece of writing in fewer words to make it concise. *Abridgement* of a document is shortening by exclusion of words without losing its sense. It may be a reduction such as practiced by *Reader's Digest* in condensing books where the language and style of the original writer is maintained.

Suppose; supposing. Both these words signify 'assumption' and in most cases are interchangeable.

> What can he do *suppose/ supposing* I don't attend the meeting?
> *Suppose/ Supposing* the minister does not turn up, the function will be held even then.

Symbols are internationally recognized representations of scientific, mathematical or measurement terms, which may be composed of letters or the alphabet or signs or symbols. Letters are used for chemical elements or measurement units and are not punctuated. It should be noted that the plural of a letter symbol is the same as the singular form. For example, the symbol for kilogram is 'kg' and it plural form remains 'kg' <u>not</u> 'kgs'; singular 'km' remains plural 'km'.

Symbols, special for computers

\	Backslash [used to separate directories and filenames]
@	Pronounced 'At' [essential symbol in e-mail ID]
_	Underscore [used in e-mail IDs]
.	Dot [*.com, .org, .in*, etc.]

Symbols for Currencies

Dollar	$
Pound sterling	£
Japanese Yen	¥
Euro	€
Frank	F

Symbols for Printing and Writing

The first six signs shown below are for directions to readers from text to footnotes in printed communication and are used in the order given]

*	Asterisk/star
†	Dagger
‡	Double dagger
§	Section mark
‖	Parallel mark
¶	Paragraph mark
@	Symbol for 'at' [commonly used in e-mail addresses]
#	Symbol for number
º	Symbol for degree
©	Copyright
™	Trade mark [written usually as superscript]
„	Ditto [-do-]

Symbols, others. Social, Literary, Spiritual, Religious and National symbols have a very wide range and scope.

Sympathy; empathy. *Sympathy* denotes 'compassion for'. The word *empathy* is sometimes used as a synonym but has another sense rather difficult to explain in a few words; it is a feeling or emotion with sensitivity or feelings of others.

> He has no *sympathy* for anyone who is punished for being late.
> Mother Teresa showed enormous *empathy* with all downtrodden people.

Synecdoche is a figure of speech which is used in two senses. In the first sense, a word for a part is used for the whole object.

> The farmer has fifty heads of cattle. [not only heads but whole cattle]
> There were ten sails to take part in the regatta. [not only sails but whole ships]
> We need ten heads at least to complete harvesting of the wheat crop in our farm. [labourers, not only their heads]

In the second sense, a word represents a whole of something but is used to stand for a part of that thing.

> In the second test, India defeated Pakistan. [only the cricket teams, not the whole countriy]

It is an American movie that is showing in the local theatre. [Hollywood produced it, not whole of America]

Synonyms are words or phrases having the same meaning. It must be realized that all synonymous words do not have exactly the same sense, the shades of meanings of the equivalent words may differ. No single word can always be used in place of another in every context. A Thesaurus is a compilation of synonymous words, and its use in conjunction with a good dictionary could contribute to writing good prose.

Syntax is the order of words in a sentence, the manner in which elements of the language as words are put together to form phrases and sentences correctly. It is a part of linguistics and grammar.

T

Take is a verb which means 'to acquire', 'to remove', 'to carry', etc. Its past tense is **took** and past participle is **taken**. Verbal phrases formed from *take* have different meanings.

> The manager could *take* the decision to down-size the work force as he had the support of the union.
> The doctor advised her to *take* the medicine thrice a day.
> The new government is to *take* office on Monday.
> They *took* refuge under a tree during the rains.
> He *took* the train to Delhi instead of flying.
> She has *taken* a job with an IT firm.
> She was *taken* ill after eating the street food.

take aback means 'to be surprised'.
> He was *taken aback* when he was asked to pay an advance of one lakh rupees.

take apart means 'to dismantle'.
> The machine was *taken apart* for thorough servicing.

take down means 'to lower' or 'to write down'.
> It is proposed to *take down* the hutment and construct a pucca building in its place.
> The secretary *took down* whatever was said in the meeting..

take in means 'to admit or include'.
> She *takes in* washing to supplement her income.

take off means 'to remove' or 'to depart'
> You have to *take off* your shoes before you enter the temple.
> The plane could *take off* only after it was thoroughly searched by the police.

take on means 'to undertake' or 'to hire'.
> After the death of her mother she *took on* the responsibility of looking after her father.

take up means 'to assume'.
> He has *taken up* the cases of the downtrodden shunned by other lawyers.

Tautology is unnecessary repetition of a word or phrase or the same idea in other words.

Common examples of tautology are:
> Attached together
> Follow after
> Follow behind

Fresh beginner
Join together
Necessary essentials
Returned back
Renew again

Teenager is not any young person, but one between the ages of 13 and 19, both inclusive, derived from numbers ending with '-teen' (thir*teen* four*teen*. fif*teen*, six*teen*, seven*teen*, eigh*teen*, and nine*teen*). It is wrong to call a twelve-year old or a twenty-year old as a teenager. The word *preteen* is used for a child nearly a teenager (generally a child between the ages of 9 and 13 by some definitions).

> She was only 10 but applied makeup like her *teenager* sister.
> As a *teenager* she wanted to have a scooter but her father bought one only when she reached the age of twenty.
> It is sad but true about some *preteen* girls getting pregnant.

Terrific; terrible are both adjectives derived from the same source meaning 'frightful' but have diverse connotations. *Terrific* is generally used in the sense of 'exciting' as a slang word. *Terrible* is derived from the original meaning. Transposition of the two words changes the meaning drastically.

> The pop concert was simply *terrific*. [excellent]
> The pop concert was simply *terrible*. [frightful]
> She drove the car at a *terrific* speed. [extraordinary]
> When we visited Manali the weather was *terrific*. [magnificent, unusually fine]
> When we visited Manali the weather was *terrible*. [frightful, very bad]
> The food served at the party was *terrific*. [very god]
> The food served at the party was *terrible*. [frightful]

That; which are pronouns that relate to objects. Though in some sentences these pronouns could be interchanged, *that* refers to things and persons, while *which* refers to things only. Either could be used to introduce restrictive clauses, but in most cases *that* serves better. Another view is *that* is to be used for a defining clause, i.e., one that conveys which one or what kind of thing one is talking about; and *which* is to be used to head a clause that amplifies the noun by giving additional information. The decision can be made on how the sentence sounds. The grammar in MS-Word also helps in making a decision.

> The family *that/ which* owns the hall rents it for marriages and other functions.
> He lives in the house *that/ which* was built by his father.
> The meditation classes *that* are held here are attended by hundreds.
> 'Gitanjali' is the work *that* brought Rabindranath Tagore the Nobel Prize.
> Uneasy lies the head *that* wears the crown.
> There is a hotel now in the palace *which* used to be the residence of the maharaja.
> I want to read 'Gitanjali' *which* brought Tagore the Nobel.

The. It is the definite article and has a different connotation from the other articles, *a* and *an*. It is also a little confusing to use and sometimes writers are in a quandary about its proper usage. Writers often use it abundance or forget to use it where required. If in doubt, it is better to judge a sentence as to how it reads with or without *the*.

The few [not many but a small number] people who attended the funeral were her admirers.
The few [a small number] shops that are in the village sell only trinkets.
The little [whatever] hope of recovery was dashed when he had the second stroke.
The little [small quantity] petrol he had in his car could only take him up to the road.

As a general guide *the* is used in a text before (a) a specific class or thing, (b) something unique, (c) a singular common noun when it denotes a whole class, (d) sobriquets of well-known people or places, (e) superlatives, (f) names of natural geographical features, (g) religious books, (h) before official titles, with or without the name, (i) for emphasis. [Capitalisation will depend on its place in the text]

(a) *The* postman brought him *a* registered letter.
   The registered letter is from *the* bank.
   The road near his home is in *a* bad condition.
   The bad condition of *the* road causes accidents.
(b) *The* sun gives us light
   The government is responsible for law and order.
   The Rashtrapati Bhawan is the official residence of *the* President of India.
(c) *The* cow's milk is good for growing children.
   The tiger is a fierce animal.
(d) *the* Lady of the Lamp (Florence Nightingale]
   the Mahatma (M. K. Gandhi)
   the City of Joy (Kolkatta)
   the Big Apple (New York City)
(e) *The* Bhuj earthquake was *the* worst in living memory.
   She gave *the* best performance of her life.
(f) *the* Ganga River
   the Mount Everest
   the Strait of Gibraltar
   the Arabian Sea
   the Indian Peninsula
(g) *the* Ramayana
   the Bible
(h) *the* President of India / *The* President Dr. A.P.J. Abdul Kalam
   the Queen
   the Prime Minister / *The* Prime Minister Mrs. Indira Gandhi
(i) *The* one and only Houdini.

She insisted that she was *the* author.

'The' before some proper place names. Normally the name of a geographical entity is a personal noun and does not take the definite article 'the'. But a few countries have 'The' (capitalised) in their official name as the names have been created from a special feature of their geography, as in the following:

The Bahamas (group of islands)
The Gambia (after the river of the same name)
The Hague
The Netherlands (after low-lying region)

Countries and regions formed by the amalgam of several diverse geographical entities also take 'the' before their names but only in a text.

the Dangs (after the tribe in Gujarat)
the Philippines (group of islands)
the Punjab (land of five rivers)
the United Arab Emirates (several emirates combined)
the United Kingdom (Great Britain and Northern Ireland)
the United States of America (Fifty states combined)

Theory; hypothesis. These two words are not synonymous; even scientists use them loosely. *Theory* is a plausible or scientifically acceptable general principle. In general parlance, it is an idea explaining something. *Hypotheses* is more tentative and implies that there is evidence, though insufficient, to provide more than uncertain explanation. A hypothesis may later become a theory after more evidence has been gathered.

The *hypothesis* of Continental Drift postulated by Alfred Wegener in 1912 is now a fully fledged *theory* after recent researches and the advent of the *Theory* of Plate Tectonics.

There. This adverb basically means 'in or that place'. It gives rise to several adverbs with different meanings.

thereabout(s) means 'near the place, or amount, or time'.
The lost dog was found near the woods or *thereabouts*.
He was paid one thousand rupees or *thereabouts* for the job.
The lights went out at midnight or *thereabout*.

thereafter means 'after that'.
The boss banged Naresh in the morning and no one had the guts to speak to him *thereafter*.

there at means 'at that' or 'at that time' or 'on that account'.
There was no quorum and the chairman postponed the meeting there at.

thereby means 'by that'.
Thereby he lost his chance to get into the team.

Thereby hangs a tale.

therefore means 'consequently'.
He has hurt his knee and *therefore* he cannot be included in the team.

therein means 'into that respect' or 'in that place'.
He is an alcoholic and *therein* lies his problem'
The information contained *therein* was useful to the police.

thereof mean 'from that cause'.
The first paragraph *thereof* clearly states that his tenancy can be terminated for late payment of the rent.

thereto means 'to that'.
The text and notes *thereto* were scrutinised before issue.

thereupon means 'immediately after that'.
Thereupon they fell on the thieves and gave them a good beating.

therewith means 'with that'.
The last item was a vote of thanks and the function ended *therewith*.

Till; Until. These two words mean nearly the same and could cause some confusion in usage. *Till* as preposition mans 'up to, or 'as late as'; as conjunction it means 'up to time when', or 'to the degree that'. *Until* is a preposition meaning 'till that time or point' or degree that', and is often used at the beginning of a sentence.
The girls pay no tuition *till* Class X.
Just wait *till* he gets his degree.
They kept on playing *till* the heavy snow blanketed the ground.
The show went on *till* the wee hours of the morning.
Until last week this was a dirt track.
You will not be allowed to go *until* you finish the work.
I am given *until* Saturday to finish the work.
The results of the election will not be available *until* tomorrow

Toward; towards. Both the words are interchangeable and mean the same: 'in the direction of' or 'as contribution to' though the latter variant is preferable..
The procession was stopped while moving *toward* the secretariat.
The contributions *toward* the cause was meager.
The thieves fled *towards* the jungle.
They have contributed *towards* raising a memorial to the fallen hero.

Turn essentially means 'to move partly or completely round'; its past tense and past participle is the same **turn'.** Verbal phrases formed from *turn* have different meanings.

turn around means 'to act abruptly' or 'to change for the better'.
After five years as a teacher she just *turned around* and left the school.
After doing all kinds of odd jobs he *turned* his life *around* and took a steady job.

turn away means 'to depart'.
> Under the influence of his guru he *turned away* from all his vices and became an ascetic.

turn back essentially means 'to return'.
> Failing to reach the summits the expedition *turned back* to the base camp.

turn down essentially means 'to reject'.
> She *turned down* the offer of promotion because it entailed shifting to a new place.

turn in means 'to go to bed' or 'hand over'.
> After a hectic day in the office it was a relief to *turn in* and go to sleep.
> He is required to *turn in* all the day's earnings to his father.

turn off means 'to shut down' or 'to discourage or offend'.
> The lights were *turned off* after the show.
> She was *turned off* by his uncouth behaviour.

turn on means 'to activate' 'to attract'.
> The lights were *turned on* in the evening.
> He was *turned on* by the scent she was wearing.

turn over means 'to deliver'.
> He *turned over* the management of the company to his son on retirement.

༺༻

U

Ultiomo. See **Idem...**

Uncle and **aunt** are two relationship terms that are very ambiguous, particularly to an Indian as Indian language words for different relationships covered in these terms are different. In English an *uncle* may be the brother of one's father or mother, or the husband of ones aunt. An *aunt* may be the sister of one's father or mother, or the wife of one's uncle. It is remarkable that a language that boasts of a vast vocabulary does not have different terms for different relationships.

Up to. It is incorrect to write it as one word 'upto'. *Up to* (preposition) is a function word to indicate continuation as far as a specified place or a limit.

> The pond is shallow and the water comes only *up to* the knees.
> It is decided that there can only be *up to* forty students in a class.

Use; utilise. Both words are synonymous to mean 'employ' or 'apply', but there is a subtle difference in usage. *Utilise* may suggest the 'discovery of a practical or productive use of something'.

> You may *use* my driveway to park your car.
> I *use* my garage to run a repair shop.
> He has put his knowledge of law to good *use*.
> She *utilises* the old utensils as flower pots. [make use of]
> I am going to *utilise* the spare time to brush up my vocabulary. [make use of]

Used to do (something); be used to doing (something). *Used to* means 'something that happened regularly' or 'went on for a time in the past'. To *be used to doing* something is 'to indicate a familiar task'.

> I *used to* play cricket in college.
> Before the fire there *used to* be a tea stall here.
> I am *used to getting up* at 5 in the morning for a morning walk.
> My son is *used to working* late hours in the office.

Valuable; invaluable. This is a case of English's peculiar word formation. Usually, when the prefix 'in-' is attached before a word it makes the word negative, like 'indirect', 'indistinct', 'insolvent' and so on. However, *valuable* (meaning 'precious' or 'of great value') is adorned with this prefix as *invaluable* it comes to mean 'priceless' which is much stronger than *valuable* in its meaning.

Verbosity is writing containing unnecessary words, that is, more words than necessary. (See **Officialese**)

In the event of his death. [if he died]
The settlement could be made *in the nature of* five hundred rupees. [about]
The answer is either in the *affirmative* or *negative*. [The answer is either 'yes' or 'no']
He *goes by the name of* Siddharth. [is called Siddharth]

Very; quite. *Very* as adverb means 'in a high degree'. *Quite* is an adverb and has the sense of 'rather' and is not as positive as *very*.

It is *very* cold here. [intensely cold]
I am *very* sure that we will win the match. [absolutely certain]
It is *quite* cold here. [cold but not much]
I am not *quite* sure that we will win the match. [there is a little element of doubt]

Vocabulary of a person is the whole body of words that a person knows. To be a successful writer, whether of a simple letter or a novel or scientific work, it is necessary to develop a vocabulary large enough to express precisely what the writer intends to convey. To develop one's vocabulary it is desirable to read any work, be it a newspaper or any other printed text, carefully and refer to a dictionary as frequently as required.

War-related words. Wars, historical and recent, have spawned words that are now a part of the vocabulary. Some examples:

Collateral damage = euphemism for civilian deaths during war.

D-day = a day set for launch of an operation (Derived from the date in 1944 on which Allied forces began the invasion of France in WW-II.)

Fifth column = enemy within (Adopted from the Spanish for organized group of sympathisers or supporters working for its enemies.)

Quisling = a traitor collaborating with the enemy. (after Major Vidkum Quisling who ruled Norway on behalf of the German occupying forces.

Shock and awe = American equivalent of German 'blitzkrieg.

Surgical strike = any damage done with precision (Derived from military jargon for precision bombing of a target sounding as if it was a medical procedure!)

Waterloo = a decisive defeat or setback (After the town in central Belgium where Napoleon was decisively defeated in 1815.)

Watergate is an office complex in Washington, DC, USA, where a series of political scandals took place in 1972 during the Presidency of Richard Nixon who had to resign afterwards. Now the suffix '-gate' is used to describe any social or political scandal.

In *Irangate*, the Regan administration sold weapons to Iran and diverted the proceeds to Contra rebels in Nicaragua. [After Iran]

In *Monicagate*, the scandal related to Monica Lewinsky's inappropriate relationship with the then US President Bill Clinton. [After Monica]

Westward; westwards; westerly; western. The correct use of the first two words is rather confusing. *Westward* is adjective and adverb both, meaning 'towards the west' and *westwards* is adverb only meaning 'in westerly direction'. Since the sense is the same, either can be used. *Westerly* has the meaning of 'in a westward position or direction' *Western* means 'situated towards or facing the south'.

> The *westward* movement of troops is to strengthen the border with Pakistan..
> If you look *westwards* you can see the faint outlines of the fort.
> The *westerly* movement of the depression brings heavy showers.
> The *western* front saw a fierce battle.

Who; whom; whose. These pronouns relating to people cause some confusion in usage. A rough and ready method for their proper usage is given here.

(1) Use *who* if the word could be replaced by 'he' 'she' or 'they'. In the following examples 'who' could be replaced by these pronouns.
>*Who* should bell the cat?
>Of the two candidates for the post *who* is the best in your opinion.
>Mr. Frank Anthony, *who* is the leader of Anglo-Indians, was nominated to Parliament.

(2) Use *whom* if the word could be replaced by 'him', her, or 'them'. In the following examples 'whom' could be replaced by these pronouns.
>The cat belongs to *whom*?
>Of the two candidates *whom* do you prefer?
>Mr. Frank Anthony is a leader of Anglo-Indians *whom* the government nominated to Parliament.

(3) Use *whose* if the word could be replaced by 'his', 'her', or 'their'. In the following sentences 'whose' could be replaced by these pronouns.
>*Whose* cat is this?
>Of the two candidates *whose* record is better in your opinion.
>Mr. Frank Anthony *whose* services to the Anglo-Indian community are well-known was nominated to Parliament.

(4) *Whose* can also be used for things where it is replaceable by 'its' or 'their'.
>Aspirin is a pain-killer *whose* efficacy to relieve migraine is doubtful.
>Goa is a preferred destination for tourist *whose* beaches are the special attraction.

Widow See **Orphan**.

With a view to... The phrase precedes some action or processes and so the gerund form of a verb ending in '-ing' is used and not the verb itself.
>He studied hard with a *view to getting* into the Civil Service. [Not 'get']
>He joined an NGO with a *view to doing* some social service. [Not 'do']
>She went to the mall with a view to buying some groceries. [Not 'buy']

Words from Legendary Place Names. There are some legendary place names that have come to describe some special attribute or quality.

Eden (Garden of) = place of delight or unspoiled beauty [from Biblical account of the abode of Adam and Eve]
>The Maldives are considered a tourist's idea of the *Garden of Eden*.

El Dorado = a place of fabulous riches [from a legendary place supposed to exist in South America]
>Minas Gerais in Brazil is quite an *El Dorado* for its fabulous deposits of precious stones.

Shangri-la = earthly paradise [from an imaginary place created by James Hilton in his novel 'Lost Horizon']
> Northern Ladakh is still a largely unexplored territory of exquisite beauty, quite a *Shangri La*!

Utopia = a place of perfect social ad political conditions [an imaginary place described in a book of the same name by Sir Thomas More] (adj., Utopian)
> Given the present status of the scheme, full literacy in the district is an *Utopian* dream.

Words from People's Names. Several words have been formed from some character displayed by an individual.

Boycott = to engage in a concerted refusal to deal with a thing or person [after a land agent in Ireland named Charles C. Boycott] (noun, verb)
> During the freedom struggle Mahatma Gandhi gave a call for *boycott* of British goods.

Chauvinism/Chauvinistic = exaggerated or blind patriotism or support of their cause [From a Napoleonic veteran Nicolas Chauvin noted for his fierce patriotism] (noun/adjective)
> Some *chauvinistic* people in Maharashtra are hounding out North Indians from Mumbai as outsiders who are taking away jobs from the locals.

Herculean = requiring or having great strength or effort [After the Greek mythological hero famed for great strength] (adjective)
> It was a *herculean* task to relocate the ancient temple to another cite from the lake formed by the dam.

Malapropism = use of absurdly misappropriate word for the word intended [After a fictional character, Mrs. Melaprop, in R. B. Sheridan's play *The Rivals*.] (noun).
> People went to him to *condone* his mother's death. [for 'condole']

Mausoleum = building erected as a tomb and monument [From ancient King Mausolus, a ruler of Caria in the Persian empire] (noun)
> Taj Mahal is the *mausoleum* built by the Mughal Emperor Shah Jahan for his queen Mumtaz Mahal.

Quixotic = foolishly impractical [From fictional Don Quixote, hero of a novel of the same name by Cervantes] (adjective)
> The scheme to link the Ganga to the river Kauvery by a canal seems to be quite *quixotic*.

Words from Place Names. Several words have been formed from some character displayed by an individual

Bohemian = a person living a socially unconventional life like an artist or writer [From a region in Czech Republic whose inhabitants are reputed to have this

attitude in life] (noun, adjective)
> The great Picasso lived a *bohemian* life not caring for the conventional modes of his times.

Marathon = something or task of long duration or an endurance contest; a footrace of 42.195 km (26 miles 385 yards) [From a place in Greece where a man ran this distance in 490 B.C. during a war] (noun)
> It was a *marathon* task to move the Abu Simbel rock-cut temples to a safer place when they were threatened inundation by Lake Nasser reservoir formed by the Aswan High Dam on the Nile.

Shanghaied = to put someone by force or trickery into a place (originally a ship) [From the past practice of shipmasters to force or trick a sailor to join an Orient-bound ship] (verb)
> First he was made unconscious by piling him high with liquor and then *shanghaied* to join the gang.

Xeno- is a prefix meaning 'foreigner' (derived from Greek *xenos*, stranger) which is used to form words such as *xenocryst* (a crystal in igneous rock not derived from the original source), *xenolith* (a fragment of rock included into another rock), and *xenophobia* (fear and hatred of foreigners or strangers).

Y

Yellow is a bright colour sometimes associated or identified with a negative implication of cowardice or jealousy. In a pejorative sense it refers to Chinese and Japanese peoples as in the phrase *the Yellow Peril* that is a danger to Western civilization. *Yellow journalism* refers to publications indulging in sensational, scandalous or distorted news. *Yellow Card* in a soccer match is shown by a referee to a player being cautioned. *Yellow Pages* is a section in a telephone or other directory devoted to listing of business and professional firms.

Yiddish words. Though not many, some words from Yuddish language are common in English usage. In a sentence they are not italicised.

Chutzpah = Audacity; conceit; nerve; supreme confidence.
> He showed great *chutzpah* and rescued the child from the burning building.

Glitch = A minor malfunction or problem.
> There was a little *glitch* and so the game started an hour late.

Kibitzer = An onlooker who often gives unwanted advice or comment, often at a card game.
> There is a *kibitzer* in our club who often spoils our game of bridge.

Kosher = Food ritually fit according to Jewish law; now in a general sense 'legitimate' or 'proper'.

There are certain practices of the society that are not *kosher*.

Yourself; himself; herself are intensive pronouns and their usage is simple as the following examples would show:
> You *yourself* suggested that I take up the job.
> I can't see why you can't cut the grass *yourself*.
> He *himself* lifted the heavy bundle
> She gave a gift to her husband and *herself* on their wedding anniversary.

Zeugma is a figure of speech in which a word applies to two others in different senses.

His licence and he *expired* last week.
The wedding *gave* him a wife and a new car on the same day.

Appendix - A

COLLECTIVE NOUNS OF ANIMALS

A menagerie of **animals**
An army/swarm of **ants**
A pace of **asses**
A colony of **bats**
A sloth of **bears**
A colony of **beavers**
A swarm/grist of **bees**
A sounder of **boars**
A swarm of **butterflies**
A string/herd/drove of **camels**
A chowder/cluster of **cats**
A herd/drove of **cattle**
A brood/flock of **chicks/chickens**
A flock/murder/muster of **crows**
A litter of **cubs**
A herd/mob of **deer**
A pack/kennel of **dogs**
A herd/drove of **donkeys**
A flock/skein/padding/team of **ducks**
A herd of **elephants**
A school/shoal of **fishes**
A swarm of **flies**
A pack/skulk of **foxes**
A gaggle/skein of **geese**
A herd of **giraffes**
A herd/flock/drove of **goats**
A band of **gorillas**
A swarm of **grasshoppers**
A group of **guinea pigs**
A down/husk of **hares**
A cast of **hawks**
A team/stud/herd of **horses**
A mute/pack of **hounds**
A swarm/plague of **insects**

A herd/troop of **kangaroos**
A kindle of **kittens**
A leap of **leopards**
A pride/troop of **lions**
A plague/swarm of **locust**
A stud of **mares**
A mob/gang of **mongoose**
A troop/swarm/hoard of **monkeys**
A watch of **nightingales**
A lock of **ostriches**
A flock of **parrots**
A covey of **partridges**
A muster of **peacocks**
A colony / rookery of **penguins**
A drove/herd of **pigs**
A flock of **pigeons**
A school of **porpoises**
A litter of **pups**
A bevy of **quails**
A nest/warren/colony of **rabbits**
A hoard of **rats**
A pod of **seals**
A flock /herd /drove of **sheep**
A host of **sparrows**
A flight of **swallows**
A flock/bevy/skein of **swans**
A colony/swarm of **termites**
A rafter of **turkeys**
A bale of **turtles**
A swarm/colony of **wasps**
A pod/gam/school of **whales**
A pack/skulk of **wolves**
A herd of **zebras.**

Appendix - B

COLLECTIVE NOUNS OF VEGETATION

A hand/bunch of **bananas**
A cluster of **branches**
A hedge of **bushes**
A sheaf/ear of **corn**
A bale of **cotton**
A bouquet/bunch/garland of **flowers**
A crate of **fruits**
A bunch of **grapes**
A tuft of **grass**
A stack of **hay**
A bundle of **sticks**
A clump/grove/copse/thicket of **trees**
An ear of **wheat**
A spring of **Paddy**

Appendix - C

COLLECTIVE NOUNS OF THINGS AND PEOPLE

A company of **actors**
A flight of **airplanes**
A peal of **bells**
A bench of **bishops**
A library of **books**
A troop of **boy scouts**
A fleet of **buses**
A fleet of **cars**
A pack/deck of **cards**
A pack of **cigarettes**
A suit of **clothes**
A troupe of **dancers**
A cluster of **diamonds**
A board of **directors**
A chest of **drawers**
A clutch/nest of **eggs**
A bunch/party of **friends**
A suite of **furniture**
A cluster of **galaxies**
A cluster of **gems**
A troop of **girl guides**
An armoury **of guns**
A cluster of **houses**
A bench of **judges**
An archipelago of **islands**
A bunch of **keys**
A gang of **labourers**
A pack/bundle of **lies/liars**
A bevy of **ladies**

A bank of (similar kinds of) **machines**
A bench of **magistrates**
A book of **mica**
A bundle of **money**
A band of **musicians**
A bundle of **nerves**
A bunch/sheaf of **papers**
A crowd of **people**
A squadron of **planes**
A team of **players**
A posse of **policemen**
A mess of **potage**
A pack of **rascals**
A crew of **sailors**
A series of **sand dunes**
A staff/army of **servants**
A fleet/armada of **ships**
A choir of **singers**
An army/platoon of **soldiers**
A cluster of **stars**
A flight of **steps**
A class of **students**
A gang of **thieves**
A set of **tools**
A fleet of **trucks**
A platoon of **waiters**
A bevy of **women**
A bale of **wool**

Appendix - D

ANIMALS: MALE, FEMALE, AND THE YOUNG

Male	Female	Young
Ass*/jack	jenny	foal
Bear*	sow	cub
Boar*/sow	kit	cub/piglet
Bull/bullock/ox	cow	calf/heifer (female)
Cat*/tom	tabby	kitten
Cock/Rooster	hen	chick/pullet
Deer*/antelope/buck	doe	fawn
Dog*	bitch	pup/puppy/whelp
Donkey*	jenny	colt/foal
Drake	duck*	duckling
Elephant*/bull	cow	calf
Fox*/dog	vixen	kit/cub/pup/puppy
Gander	goose*	gosling
	Goat*/billy she-goat/nanny	kid
Horse*/stallion	mare	foal/colt (male)/filly (female)
King	queen	prince (male); princess (female)
Lion	lioness	cub/whelp
Owl	hen (?)	owlet
Panther	pantheress	cub
Peacock	peahen	chick
Pig*/swine/hog/boar	sow	piglet
Rabbit*/buck rabbit	doe	bunny
Sheep*/ram	ewe	lamb/lambkin
Stag/hart	hind	fawn
Swan*/cob	pen	cygnet
Tiger*	tigress	cub
Wolf*	she wolf	cub

* The general/common name of the species

Appendix - E

ANMAL SOUNDS

Asses bray
Bears growl
Bees hum
Birds sing chirp / twitter / warble
Bulls / oxen bellow
Camels grunt
Cats mew / purr
Cattle low
Cocks crow
Cows low
Crows caw
Dogs bark / howl / yelp
Doves coo
Ducks quack
Elephants trumpet
Flies buzz
Foxes yelp
Frogs croak
Geese cackle

Goats bleat
Hens cluck / cackle
Horses neigh
Jackals howl
Kittens mew / purr
Lambs bleat
Lions roar
Mice squeak
Monkeys chatter / gibber
Owls hoot / screech
Parrots talk
Pigeons coo
Snakes/serpents hiss
Sheep bleat
Squirrels squeak
Tigers roar / grow
Vultures scream
Wolves howl

Appendix - F

PHOBIAS

Phobia is an exaggerated and illogical fear of a particular object or class of object or situation. There are several kinds of phobias and each has a special term to describe it. A selection of terms for common phobias is given here.

Alcohol	methyphobia / potophobia
Alone	autopobhobia / monophobia
Ants	myrmecophobia
Bees	apiphobia / malissophobia
Blood	homophobia / hemaphobia / hematophobia
Bridges, crossing them	gephyrophobia
Buildings, in being close to	betaphobia
Car or vehicle riding	amaxophobia
Confined spaces	claustrophobia
Crossing street	agyrophobia / dromo
Dark places, being in	lygophobia
Darkness	achlnophiobia / myctophobia / scotophobia
Death or dying	thanotophobia
Dentist	dentophobia
Depth	bathophobia
Dog	cynophobia
Electricity	electrophobia
Fire	pyrophobia / arsonphobia
Fish	ichthyphobia
Flowers	anthrophobia
Flying	aviophobia / aviatophobia / pteromerhansphobia
Foreigner	xenophobia
Fur or skin of animals	doraphobia
Heights	acrophobia / altophobia / batophobia hypsephobia hyposo
Hospitals	nosocomephobia
Injections	typonophobia

Insects	acrophobia entophobia insectophobia
Lightening and thunder	brontophobia karauno
Mice	musophobia monophobia suriphobia
Mobs and crowds	demophobia enochlophbia orchlophobia
Noise	acousticophobia
Number 13	triskaidekaphoba
Ocean and sea	thalassophobia
Train travel	siderodromophobia
Reptile	herpetophobia
Snow	chionophobia
Sound	acousticophobia
Spider	arachnophobia
Termites	isopetrophobia
Water	hydrophobia
Worms	scoleciphobia

Appendix - G

MANIAS

Mania is excessive or unreasonable enthusiasm for any object. Several types of mania are recognised and some common ones are noted here.

Ablutomania	excessive desire for washing oneself
Agromania	intense desire to be in open spaces
Aphrodiscomania	abnormal sexual interest
Bibliomania	craze for books and reading
Dipsomania	abnormal craving for alcohol
Discomania	obsession for disco music
Ergosomania/ergomania	excessive desire to work
Eratomania	abnormally powerful sex desire
Graptomania	obsession for working/workaholic
Kleptomania	irrational predilection for stealing
Melomania	craze for music

Methomania	morbid craving for alcohol
Musomania	obsession with music
Necromania	sexual obsession with dead bodies/necrophilia
Oniomania	excessive desire for making purchases
Phagomania	excessive desire for food or eating
Phaneromania	habit of biting one's finger nails
Plutomania	excessive craving for money
Pseudomania	irrational predilection for lying
Sebastomania	religious insanity
Verbomania	craze for words

Appendix - H

FIELDS & BRANCHES OF KNOWLEDGE

Discipline	*Study/Science of...*
Acoustics	sound [Physics]
Agronomy	soil management and crop production [Agriculture]
Algebra	arithmetic in which letters and other symbols are used to represent numbers in formulas [Mathematics]
Anthropology	humankind
Archaeology	human prehistory and antiquities
Arithmetic	manipulation of numbers (addition, subtraction, multiplication, division) [Mathematics]
Astronomy	heavenly bodies
Astrophysics	physical nature of stars and other celestial objects [Astronomy]
Bacteriology	bacteria [Medicine, Biology]
Biography	written life of a person
Biology	physical life of plants and animals
Botany	plants
Calculus	higher method of calculation [Mathematics]
Cardiology	action and diseases of heart [Medicine]
Cartography	drawing maps
Chemistry	elements and compounds and all matter
Cosmogony	origin of universe, especially the solar system

Cosmology	origin and development of the universe
Criminology	crime and criminals
Crystallography	crystals [Physics; Geology]
Cytology	structure and function of plant and animal cells [Biology]
Demography	structure of human population [Geography]
Dermatology	concerned with skin disorders [Medicine]
Ecology	interrelation of organisms and their environments [Biology]
Electronics	concerned with behaviour of electrons [Physics]
Economics	concerned with production and trade of goods and services.
Endocrinology	endocrine glands [Medicine, Physiology]
Entomology	insects [Zoology]
Epigraphy	ancient inscriptions [Archaeology]
Ethnography	peoples and their culture [Anthropology]
Ethnology	characteristics of different peoples and their relationships
Gastroenterology	diseases of stomach and intestines [Medicine]
Genetics	heredity and variation of organisms [Biology]
Geodesy	the shape and area of the Earth [Mathematics]
Geography	physical features the Earth and of human activities
Geology	Earth's crust
Geometry	properties and relations of magnitude in space [Mathematics]
Gemmology	gems and precious stones
Genetics	heredity and inherited characters [Biology]
Geodesy	shape and area of the Earth and its large parts [Mathematics, Geophysics]
Geomorphology	physical features of the Earth's surface [Geology, Geography]
Geophysics	physics of the Earth
Geriatrics	health and welfare of old people [Medicine]
Gerontology	process of aging and its problems [Medicine]
Gynecology	specific disease of female humans [Medicine]
Haematlogy	physiology of the blood [Medicine]
Hagiography	written life of a saint or biography in praise of a person
Histology	microscopic structure of tissues [Biology]
Historiography	writing of history and of written histories
Horology	measurement of time and making of clocks and watches
Hydrology	properties and distribution of water on the Earth's surface
Immunology	resistance to infection and immune systems [Medicine, Biology]

Indology	Indian history, literature, philosophy, etc.
Limnology	lakes and other fresh-water bodies [Geography, Geology]
Linguistics	languages and their structure
Mathematics	numbers and their operations and of space
Metallurgy	extracting metals from ore and their working
Meteorology	weather and atmosphere
Microbiology	micro-organisms (animals and plants)
Mineralogy	minerals [Geology]
Museology	museum organization and management
Musicology	music (as an academic subject)
Mycology	fungi [Botany]
Nephrology	physiology and diseases of kidney [Medicine]
Neurology	nervous system [Medicine; Biology]
Numismatics	coins and medals
Oceanography	oceans and seas
Oncology	tumours (and cancers) [Medicine]
Ophthalmology	diseases of the eye [Medicine]
Optics	behaviour of light [Physics]
Ornithology	birds [Zoology]
Orography	physical study of mountains [Geography]
Orthopaedics	bones and muscles [Medicine]
Palaeobotany	fossil (extinct) plants [Geology]
Palaeontology	fossil (extinct) organisms [Geology]
Palynology	pollen grains and other spores [Botany]
Pathology	causes and effects of diseases [Medicine]
Pedagogy	teaching or education
Pediatrics	diseases of children [Medicine]
Pedology	soils [Agriculture, Geology, Geography]
Petrology	rocks [Geology]
Pharmacology	uses, effects and action of drugs [Medicine]
Philately	postage stamps and their collection
Philology	structure, development and relationship of languages
Phonetics	speech sounds
Physics	nature and properties of matter and energy
Physiology	function and phenomenon of living things [Biology]
Phytology	plants (obsolete name for Botany)
Posology	drug dosage [Medicine]
Proctology	diseases of anus and rectum [Medicine]

Psychiatry	mental, emotional and behavioral disorders [Medicine]
Psychology	human mind and its behaviour
Pteridology	ferns and related plants [Botany]
Radiology	x-rays and high energy radiation [Medicine]
Sedimentology	sedimentary rocks [Geology]
Seismology	earthquakes [Geology; Geophysics]
Silviculture	development and care of forests
Sinology	Chinese culture, language and history
Sociology	development, structure and functioning of human society
Speleology	caves [Geology, Geography]
Statistics	collecting and analysis of numerical data [Mathematics]
Stratigraphy	order and relative dating of Earth's strata [Geology]
Systematics	concerned with classification and nomenclature of living beings [Biology]
Taxonomy	classification of biota [Biology]
Thermodynamics	relation between heat and other forms of energy in physical and chemical processes [Chemistry, Physics]
Theology	religion
Topology	geometrical properties and spatial relations [Mathematics]
Trigonometry	properties of triangles [Mathematics]
Urology	urinary systems [Medicine]
Virology	viruses [Medicine, Biology]
Volcanoloy	volcanoes [Geology, Geography]
Zoology	animals

www.ingramcontent.com/pod-product-compliance
Lightning Source LLC
Chambersburg PA
CBHW080552230426
43663CB00015B/2808